Group Dynamics in the Language Classroom

CAMBRIDGE LANGUAGE TEACHING LIBRARY

A series covering central issues in language teaching and learning, by authors who have expert knowledge in their field.

In this series:

Group Dynamics in the Language Classroom

Zoltán Dörnyei
and
Tim Murphey

CAMBRIDGE
UNIVERSITY PRESS

PUBLISHED BY THE PRESS SYNDICATE OF THE UNIVERSITY OF CAMBRIDGE
The Pitt Building, Trumpington Street, Cambridge, United Kingdom

CAMBRIDGE UNIVERSITY PRESS
The Edinburgh Building, Cambridge CB2 2RU, UK
40 West 20th Street, New York, NY 10011–4211, USA
477 Williamstown Road, Port Melbourne, VIC 3207, Australia
Ruiz de Alarcón 13, 28014 Madrid, Spain
Dock House, The Waterfront, Cape Town 8001, South Africa

http://www.cambridge.org

© Cambridge University Press 2003

This book is in copyright. Subject to statutory exception
and to the provisions of relevant collective licensing agreements,
no reproduction of any part may take place without
the written permission of Cambridge University Press.

First published 2003
Reprinted 2004

Printed in the United Kingdom at the University Press, Cambridge

Typeface Sabon 10.5/12pt. *System* 3B2 [CE]

A catalogue record for this book is available from the British Library

Library of Congress Cataloguing in Publication data applied for

ISBN 0521 82276 9 hardback
ISBN 0521 52971 9 paperback

BLACKBURN COLLEGE
LIBRARY

Acc. No. BB15612
HSC
Class No. 418.007 DOR

Date 07|03|08

Contents

Preface: How we came to write this book

Why would a Hungarian living in Britain and an American living in the Far East – both practising language teacher-researchers – decide to write a book together? And why on 'group dynamics' of all topics? Here are our personal accounts:

Zoltán

As a practising language teacher I often felt that the field of psychology had a lot to offer me on how to teach better. This is why when I decided to do postgraduate work in the area, I selected a psychological topic, the role of motivation in foreign language learning. During my studies I spent a lot of time in libraries trying to trace down various literature leads and references that I came across in my reading. One such lead suggested that student motivation was sometimes influenced by the learner group – something every student knows who has worried about getting along with his or her new peers. Before long, I realised that groups did much more than just 'pull down' or 'up' a learner. They have a life of their own and – to my great surprise – this life had been the subject of a whole subdiscipline within the social sciences called *group dynamics*. My next surprise came when I found out that this vigorous and, from an educational point of view, extremely relevant subdiscipline was virtually unknown in the second language (L2) field, so I quickly added a chapter to my dissertation describing its basic principles.

Then I got along with my life, focusing mainly on motivation research, but group dynamics was always in the back of my mind as one of the potentially most promising areas to explore; I even wrote a few smaller articles on it (Dörnyei 1990; Dörnyei and Gajdátsy 1989a, 1989b). In the early 1990s, I met a wonderful person, Angi Malderez, who came to work in Hungary at my university. As it turned out, she had also been hooked by group dynamics and had even started to write a book on it with a friend, Jill Hadfield, some years back. Although life in the end took them to different parts of the world and it was Jill who completed the book alone (Hadfield 1992), Angi, just like me, became a group enthusiast. We decided to pool our experiences and produced a review paper, which, to our dismay, was at first misunderstood by most journal reviewers. It appeared that they simply did not see the point in looking at group dynamics, often mistaking 'group dynamics' for 'group work' and referring us to Long and Porter's well-known 1985 paper on the usefulness of student interaction for language acquisition.

I was about to give up when one day, out of the blue, I received a letter from Earl Stevick who had been one of the reviewers of our manuscript and who was upset that it had been rejected. He encouraged us to keep trying, and this encouragement – coupled with the subtle change in the zeitgeist in the field (with psychological approaches gaining prominence) – finally brought results: Angi and I succeeded in publishing not one but two overviews of the field (Dörnyei and Malderez 1997, 1999), and a summary of group dynamics and co-operative learning (Dörnyei 1997) was also accepted in a special issue of the *Modern Language Journal*, edited by Martha Nyikos and Rebecca Oxford (1997). To top it off, an American colleague, Madeline Ehrman, and I decided to write a theoretical summary of group dynamics and group psychology, which the American publisher Sage contracted straight away (Ehrman & Dörnyei 1998).

Thus, by the end of the 1990s there were two books out on group dynamics in the L2 field: Jill Hadfield's (1992) very practical guide and Ehrman & Dörnyei's (1998) highly theoretical work. What was missing was something in between: a book promoting group dynamics that would contain a more elaborate rationale and overview than the Hadfield book (which, apart from short introductions, only offers classroom activities in a 'recipe book format') but would be more accessible and relevant to classroom practitioners than the Ehrman-Dörnyei monograph. So I was on the lookout to find a fellow enthusiast who would be happy to join this project – after all, the best way to write about groups is surely in a team!

I have known Tim for a long time and I always thought that he was one of the most creative applied linguists, constantly coming up with original and highly colourful ideas. He also has the rare gift of being able to combine an interest in some of the most theoretical issues of the field and a passion for actual classroom teaching. One day, after I had already moved from Hungary to Britain, I was reading Tim's entertaining and thought-provoking book, *Language Hungry! An introduction to language learning fun and self-esteem* (Murphey 1998a), and it suddenly clicked: Tim would be the ideal companion for the group project. And before long, we were on the way.

Tim

Groups, teams and communities have often excited me with their potential for greater learning, amazed me with their increased creativity, and sometimes disappointed me with their failure to communicate and come together. For the first seven years of my career at the University of Florida's English Language Institute I taught diverse groups of international students (Asians, Arabs, Latin Americans, and Europeans), followed by eight years teaching and doing my PhD research on music and song in language education in Neuchatel, Switzerland. As a grad student, I partially supported myself by teaching private lessons and wrote *Teaching One to One* (1991), which looks closely at building rapport with others. During this period, I also worked for 15 summers as a language and sports teacher to international children from six to seventeen years of age in the Swiss Alps, forming groups in and out of the classroom. Then came 11 years at a Japanese university and a year and a half in Taiwan before returning to Japan in 2003. (Don't add all those up!) In every environment, with whatever the mix of cultures, I have found that explicitly attending to group-forming processes and stages has paid off in more peaceful classrooms and improved learning.

As pleasurable as some of my own classes have been, I still want to understand better how to consistently bring people together, excite them with the greater possibilities of cohesive teams, and navigate the inevitable ups and downs of group life. I see threads of this in my own writing about friends (Murphey 1998b), near peer role models (Murphey 1998c; Murphey and Arao 2001), and critical collaborative autonomy (Murphey and Jacobs 2000). While in Switzerland doing my PhD, I lived in a community of students who ardently discussed and debated practically everything. I was introduced to, and enacted, the Vygotskian idea that learning appears first in social interaction, between minds, and that messages are co-constructed by participants. About 15 years later, another group exemplified this process for me even more dramatically: Mark Clarke's 'doctoral lab' at the University of Colorado, Denver. Composed of about a dozen 'as diverse as you've ever seen' highly social thinkers who delighted in exploring ideas systemically, they welcomed me openly for three months when I was on sabbatical in 1999 and showed me the essentials of a high-achieving group: food, fun, friendliness, flexibility and ferocious philosophising with a purpose!

As I began to work on this project with Zoltán in 2001, I was changing jobs from Nanzan University in Japan to Yuan Ze University in Taiwan, saying goodbye to several groups and wondering how I was going to fit in with new faculty, students and cultures. I was a bit anxious about leaving the 'known' and learning a bit of Chinese, and at the same time also excited. Now, as we are finishing this book, I am planning my return to Japan in April 2003 to Dokkyo University, and again saying goodbye to groups that I have become very attached to and again feeling the anxiety and excitement that comes with joining new groups. Thus, writing this book at this moment in my life has been doubly rewarding because I have been able to use what we are writing about even more deeply as I am travelling between cultures, countries and institutions. In fact, I believe that because of this book, I have recently been able to have some of the most powerfully cohesive groups I have ever had.

While much of the early research in group dynamics was Western in origin and often in business contexts, I and my graduate students (junior and senior high school teachers) have found group dynamics extremely relevant in our Asian educational environments (Murphey 2003; Ozawa 2002). My energetic MA graduate school class in Taiwan read this book in draft form and daringly tried out suggestions in their own language classes. While, stereotypically, Asia is known for its cohesive groups, we found that actually studying how groups form and perform could take us beyond superficial social groups and help us construct more high performing teams. More recently, I have shared this information in training workshops in Syria and received similarly positive reactions.

I had read several of Zoltán's articles and books before I actually met him on a trip to Budapest back in the early 1990s. Since then we have met at numerous conferences, always interested in each other's research. It has been exciting to work on this book with him. He has a contagious enthusiasm for his research and teaching, and is an easy person to immediately like. Over a delicious breakfast at a very old train station halfway between the East and West in February 2001, we decided this would be a wonderful book to write together. And it has been!

Introduction

The topic of this book – *group dynamics* – may sound like one of those very scientific terms that are impressive but which no one understands. This is not surprising: before we came across the concept, almost by accident, we had had only a very vague idea about what it could mean. And although now both of us are convinced that group dynamics is probably one of the most – if not *the* most – useful subdisciplines in the social sciences for language teachers, it is still virtually unknown in second language (L2) research.

Therefore, we believe that before we embark on our exploration of the field, we owe you some initial explanation. In this introductory chapter we would like to address three questions that we would ask if we were readers of this book. These are:

- What is group dynamics and why is it important for language teachers?
- Why is 'group dynamics' such an unknown concept in L2 studies and where can we find more information?
- What will be learned in this book and how will it help our teaching?

Invitation to participate

Before we answer these questions, let us briefly talk about you, the 'reader-thinker-reflective teacher'. We have written this book for a relatively wide audience that would include would-be and practising teachers, methodologists, teacher educators and applied linguists, but we would expect everybody who decides to spend some time with this book to share one thing in common: an interest in the language learning/teaching process within a classroom context. So we assume that whatever your current position, you consider yourself (at least partly) a language teacher at heart.

As we will argue, group dynamics is more than a domain of

knowledge (i.e. rules and principles); it also involves a general group-sensitive approach and attitude. So that you can share these more personal aspects, we invite you to join us, to reflect and to add your experiences to the discussions. You have certainly been involved with many groups, teams and classes, and will have noticed yourself some effective elements of group dynamics. Your own past experience, while perhaps seldom considered within the light of group dynamics, is a great source of information. We encourage you to draw on it and thereby enrich and expand on what we say.

> **Think about it first**
>
> Remember some groups that you really liked belonging to. What were their qualities? Then remember a few that were not so good, or were outright terrible. What were the differences? What do you think makes a good group and a not so good group?

Throughout this book we are going to tell many personal stories and allow many other people's voices to be heard, trying to create a kind of community within a book. We hope you will examine the ideas we present critically and compare them to your own life experiences. This is particularly important because the relevance of the principles and strategies that we will present greatly depends on the cultural and institutional context you work in. Therefore, we would like to invite you to continuously explore the applicability of the material with regard to your own school context. Given the diversity of language teaching situations worldwide, it is unlikely that everything we say will be directly relevant to your own teaching. What works in one location might be a recipe for failure in another. Although between the two of us we have had some teaching experience in a number of countries in Europe, the US and East Asia, we are not under the illusion that we have 'seen it all', and no matter how hard we have tried to avoid any cultural, social or gender bias, some might still be unintentionally here. Please bear this in mind when you come across something in this book which you think is culturally biased or which does not make any sense from your perspective.

> **Reflection**
>
> Ask the people around you casually, 'Are you currently a member of a "good" group? Or do you teach a "good" group?' And if the answer is positive, 'Is this a common thing in your life/teaching? What made this group good? How did it happen?'

What is group dynamics and why is it important for language teachers?

There are two simple but basic facts that have led to the formation of the subdiscipline of group dynamics within the social sciences which has the explicit objective of studying groups:

1. Groups have been found to have a 'life of their own' – that is, individuals in groups behave differently from the way they do outside the group (which is reflected, for example, when we say that someone has got into 'bad company').
2. Although groups vary in size, purpose, composition and character, even the most different kinds of groups appear to share some fundamental common features, making it possible to study 'the group' in general.

Inspired by these observations, the systematic study of groups was initiated in the United States by social psychologist Kurt Lewin and his associates in the 1940s, and literally thousands of research papers and monographs have been written on the topic ever since. Group dynamics is a vigorous and vibrant field, overlapping various branches of psychology and sociology, and, as you can imagine, there is also a lot of interest in its results within industry and business (e.g. the study of management teams), psychotherapy (e.g. group therapy) and even politics (e.g. the nature of political leadership and decision-making). Currently, the field is experiencing a renaissance: as Levine and Moreland (1998) conclude in the *Handbook of Social Psychology*, during the past 15 years interest in groups has increased markedly amongst scholars, as indicated by the number of pages devoted to research on groups in the major academic journals.

One of the reasons for the widespread interest in groups is the recognition that a group has greater resources than any single member alone – an observation that has also been expressed in proverbs in many cultures (e.g. the Kenyan proverb, 'Sticks in a bundle are unbreakable', or the English proverb, 'Many hands make light work'). Indeed, the 'TEAM' acronym says it all: 'Together Everyone Achieves More'. The basic assumption of this book is that group dynamics is also relevant to educational contexts because the class group can have a significant impact on the effectiveness of learning:

- In a 'good' group, the L2 classroom can turn out to be such a pleasant and inspiring environment that the time spent there is a constant source of success and satisfaction for teachers and learners alike. And even if someone's commitment should flag, his or her peers are likely to 'pull the person along' by providing the necessary motivation to persist.

- In contrast, when something 'goes wrong' with the class – for example conflicts or rebellious attitudes emerge, or there is sudden lethargy or complete unwillingness for cooperation on the students' part – the L2 course can become a nightmare. Teaching is hard if not impossible and even the most motivated learners lose their commitment. Does the following extract ring a bell?

From an interview with a student

I: *Do you remember something about the bad group?*

A: *Kids getting late to class and leaving early, people sleeping in the class, and talking about all kinds of crazy things, and girls brushing their hair, doing their nails . . . and not looking at the teacher at all, and I would feel really bad, and I would look at the teacher and the teacher wouldn't see because he wouldn't look at the students . . .* (Adapted from Costa Guerra 2002)

What causes these differences? Why do some classes feel 'good' and some 'bad' at different times or all the time? What is it about certain learner groups which makes them appropriate or inappropriate learning environments? In *Group Dynamics in the Language Classroom* we argue that it is largely the dynamics of the learner group – i.e. its internal characteristics and its evolution over time – that determine the climate of the classroom. This learner group, made up of the teacher as the central figure and the students as active members, is a powerful social unit, which is in many ways bigger than the sum of its parts. If group development goes astray, it can become a serious obstacle to learning and can 'punish' its members by making group life miserable. However, when positive group development processes are attended to, they can reward the group's members and can provide the necessary driving force to pursue group learning goals beyond our expectations. Earl Stevick (1980) has summarised this point succinctly when he stated that in a language course 'success depends less on materials, techniques and linguistic analyses, and more on what goes on inside and between the people in the classroom' (p. 4).

Why indeed . . . ?

'But why should we pay attention to group processes? Isn't our job simply to teach efficiently? Surely the group process can look after itself? The way the students relate to each other is not the teacher's business; the teacher's business is to transmit content, and whether

---

the class gets on with each other is irrelevant. However, that is not the message I got from the cries of misery from staffrooms all over Britain, and I am convinced that a successful group dynamic is a vital element in the teaching/learning process.'

(Jill Hadfield 1992:10)

Why is 'group dynamics' such an unknown concept in L2 studies and where can we find more information?

Having read the above section, you would be quite right to ask, 'If this is all true, why is group dynamics so unknown in language education? How come few have thought about these things before?' To add to your puzzlement, it is not only language education where group dynamics is virtually unknown but this is true of the whole domain of education. Why is this?

The honest answer is that we don't know. Of course, we can think of several possible reasons:

- Group dynamics researchers do not like to talk about educational contexts because in most schools it is difficult to find proper 'groups'. It's not that there are no groups, but just the opposite: there are too many of them and they overlap considerably. In most schools in the world, class group membership fluctuates continuously: the group is regularly split up into smaller independent units based on gender (e.g. when boys and girls are taught physical education separately), competence (e.g. half of the class studies a language at a more advanced level), or interest (e.g. various specialisation tracks). It is also common that for certain classes some other students join the group; and even with fairly stable class groups, at least one key member – the teacher – may change regularly, according to the subject matter. Thus, in such an environment it is difficult to define what the 'primary group' is, which might be the reason why we are aware of only one single work that covers this subject – *Group Processes in the Classroom* by Richard and Patricia Schmuck (2001) – although this book is already on its 8th edition . . .
- For reasons unknown to us, university teacher education programmes all over the world tend to specialise on subject-matter training, and far less attention is paid to practical (educational), let alone psychological, issues. So, if you want to obtain, say, an English teaching degree, you are more likely to have to study Shakespeare or generative syntax than the psychological foundation of the classroom. And even in practical teacher training courses organised outside the university

system, the useful insights and suggestions provided are only very rarely accompanied by a more theoretical justification of group dynamics.

- In language education and applied linguistics, the problem is further augmented by the fact that hardly any high-profile specialists and theoreticians have a background in psychology, and therefore a domain such as group dynamics is usually outside their scope or interest.

Christopher Brumfit on the need to understand groups – almost 20 years ago!

'. . . any use of language by small groups in the classroom requires learners to operate with a great deal more than language alone, for other semiotic systems will come into play, and personal and social needs will be expressed and responded to, simply as a result of the presence of several human beings together for a cooperative purpose. But the ways in which these systems interact have not been systematised by researchers . . .' (Brumfit 1984:74)

Luckily, modern language education has raised awareness about group issues: after all, communicative teaching activities often require *small group work* and active *interaction* among the students, which would be very difficult to achieve if, say, the class was split up into cliques who did not communicate with each other. Therefore, there has recently been an increasing amount of published material in the L2 field on groups and student relations that you can turn to for additional information. We have summarised the works we have found most useful in the Further reading box below.

Further reading

If you are interested in practical aspects of group dynamics in language education, we would recommend Jill Hadfield's (1992) pioneering book, *Classroom Dynamics*. This is an excellent practical book, offering a collection of interactive group-building language activities that are accessible and easy to apply. A more theoretical overview can be found in Madeline Ehrman and Zoltán Dörnyei's (1998) *Interpersonal Dynamics in Second Language Education: The Visible and Invisible Classroom*, which provides a comprehensive synthesis of research in this area.

Although the two works above are the only available books in

---

the L2 field specifically targeting group issues, we can find some shorter discussions in journal articles or book chapters, and a number of related issues have also received increased attention during the past decade. Articles addressing general group-related questions include Dörnyei and Malderez (1997, 1999) and Senior (1996, 1997, 2002). Cooperative language learning, which is a small-group-based instructional approach built on the principles of group dynamics, has also been analysed by a growing body of literature (for a review, see a special issue of the *Modern Language Journal* edited by Nyikos and Oxford 1997). To learn more about the issue of the teacher as a facilitator, please refer to Underhill (1999) and Stevick (1990). Practical 'warmer' and 'icebreaker' activities have been offered by several teachers' resource books, e.g. Frank and Rinvolucri (1991), Malderez & Bodóczky (1999) and Maley and Duff (1982). Other L2-specific works that contain material relevant to group dynamics include Arnold (1999), Brumfit (1984), Legutke and Thomas (1994), Murphey (2001a), Murphey and Jacobs (2000) and Williams and Burden (1997).

Outside the L2 field, we find an abundance of group-related materials, particularly with a non-educational focus. As mentioned earlier, Schmuck and Schmuck (2001) is the only comprehensive overview of group dynamics in the classroom. However, several classroom management handbooks also cover group issues – Jones and Jones (2000) is a classic, already on its 6th edition. We would also recommend Tiberius's (1999) very useful trouble-shooting guide to small group teaching.

Within the actual field of group dynamics, the most comprehensive summary is provided by Forsyth (1999) – which again is regularly updated (it is now on its 3rd edition) – and Brown (2000) is also on the way to becoming a classic (now on its 2nd edition). Johnson and Johnson's (2000) seminal text on group theory and group skills (already on its 7th edition) also has a lot of relevant materials. Two recently published texts that we have found illuminating are Levi (2001) and Oyster (2000) – the latter is particularly refreshing with its good sense of humour. Finally, a sub-area of communication studies – *small group communication* – also displays significant overlaps with group dynamics; a classic text (already on its 6th edition) that we have used is Wilson (2002).

What will we learn in this book and how will it help our teaching?

The objective of this book is to promote a wider understanding of the principles of group dynamics in the language teaching profession. On the one hand, we have intended this to be a practical book that brings group dynamics to life by relating it to real classrooms, including frequent illustrative materials and quoting a range of different 'voices' talking about groups, such as teachers, students and researchers. On the other hand, we would also like to provide systematic discussion of the major issues and tenets of the field. There is a well-known (and perhaps too-often-quoted) saying, attributed to Kurt Lewin, which states that 'There is nothing so practical as a good theory.' Both of us have personally experienced the truth of this claim and believe that even when our aim is to achieve an understanding of the practical aspects of a certain topic, it is important to have an overview of it. Thus, in the following chapters we will invite you to consider and explore:

- the most important group characteristics;
- the main stages of group development;
- the various functions and features of different leadership styles (after all, every teacher is, by definition, a group leader).

We will also address very practical points such as:

- how to handle conflicts;
- how to increase friendship amongst the students;
- how to make the class more goal-oriented.

And we will elaborate on abstract but highly useful terms such as:

- group cohesiveness;
- group norms;
- group structure.

Will knowing about all this help actual teaching? We think so. In fact, we feel group dynamics is at the heart of teaching anything. Our suggestions come from our own experience of teaching with an increased awareness about group dynamics. This awareness has made us more confident and, we believe, more successful teachers. We have watched group after group through the lens of group dynamics and implemented the ideas we suggest in these pages. We have seen disparate students become cohesive supporting groups of individuals, daring to push the limits of their own development. Several ways of creating positive group dynamics are simple, effective and easy to implement, provided we realise their potential. And while bigger group dynamics issues that help us to understand classroom events may need more attention, they certainly do not require scientists and researchers to 'decode' them. At the end of each chapter, we will summarise the most important aspects in accessible group-building strategies and suggestions, and we will list these all together in the concluding chapter.

Let us just say one more thing by way of recommendation: we have found that group dynamics is a genuinely *interesting* discipline. It is a bit like peeping behind the curtains and finding out a hidden dimension of a familiar thing, in our case the language classroom.

Will it work in your school?

One of the reviewers of the manuscript of this book has warned us that some readers might be inclined to dismiss the content of this book as a mere 'luxury' that teachers who do not work in privileged circumstances simply cannot afford to attend to. Yes, we can see that an overburdened practitioner whose main job is to get large classes through a number of language exams might find it more difficult to implement our ideas than others working in a more permissive environment. Yet this does not so much raise questions about the overall validity of group processes as about educational change and school reform in general. We truly sympathise with colleagues who work in school situations in which many group-building strategies seem unrealistic. But we hope that even they will find some manageable ideas and further inspiration in the following pages. We will return to this question in a section in the concluding chapter that highlights the need to consider the whole school environment.

The importance of spending time on group dynamics

The successful business management consultant and writer Steven Covey (1989:151) introduces a 'Time Management Matrix' as a useful tool to help to increase self-awareness and effectiveness. The matrix (see overleaf) uses four criteria to describe things we do: along the side, Covey puts 'Important' and 'Not Important', and on the top he puts 'Urgent' and 'Not Urgent'. He then lists activities that are typically done in each of these spaces.

	URGENT	NOT URGENT
IMPORTANT	*(Space 1)* Crises Pressing problems Deadline-driven projects	*(Space 2)* Prevention, PC activities Relationship building Recognising new opportunities Planning, recreation
NOT IMPORTANT	*(Space 3)* Interruptions, some calls Some mail, some reports Some meetings Proximate, pressing matters Popular activities	*(Space 4)* Trivia Some mail Some phone calls Time wasters Pleasant activities

Covey argues that any one of the four quadrants can become bigger and bite into the time of the others. When the Important/Urgent quadrant (Space 1) is dominant, we seem to continually be putting out fires and can burn out. On the other hand, if we spend a great deal of time on Important/Not Urgent activities (Space 2), this tends to reduce the number and severity of the fires that occur in the first place. Those who concentrate on Not Important/Urgent activities (Space 3) are not understanding goals and plans and have a short-term focus. And finally those whose activities are mostly in the Not Important/Not Urgent quadrant (Space 4) are irresponsible, depend on others a lot, and may often get fired.

Most group building activities belong to the Important/Not Urgent quadrant of the matrix, in Space 2. Below we have created a simplified grid for teachers from the point of view of group dynamics; we only included the Important row, even though we are aware how much time and energy we tend to spend on not important activities nowadays, such as red tape. The results of concentrating on each of the two 'spaces' are:

- *Important/Urgent:* Stress and burnout; frequent crisis management/ putting out fires; being 'on the run'; often feeling exhausted.
- *Important/Not Urgent:* Calmer state; fewer and less severe crises; balance; improved quality of life; time to just be there; often feeling energised; job satisfaction.

Thus, the point we would like to make is that we sincerely believe that the more time we invest in the Important/Not Urgent activities, the less we need to worry about crisis management. It will give us more time to look more closely at the quality of teaching rather than continually putting out management fires. Learning about group dynamics and organising well-functioning groups will go a long way toward facilitating smooth classroom management and enhancing student performance. Looking at the teaching task matrix below, how much time would you estimate that you spend in each of these two spaces normally?

	URGENT	NOT URGENT
IMPORTANT	*(Space 1)* Using discipline and control strategies (controlling distracting students and stopping arguments) Finding short-term solutions 'Fast food' class preparation Combating student apathy	*(Space 2)* Socialisation Community/group building Planning, seeing the big picture Engendering motivation Teacher development

Some people who live in Space 1 justify it by saying they have to stay there to keep the wheels turning and they accuse people in Space 2 of being egocentric for taking time to go and develop themselves. We feel that when you choose to spend time in Space 2, it is far from egocentric; the healthy construction of ourselves and of cohesive groups in our classes demand that we spend quality time in Space 2. Of course, none of us lives in any one space all the time. But we need to step back every once in a while and reconsider how we might improve the quality of our lives. This is a Space 2 book.

1 Becoming a group

This chapter will:

- *discuss what a 'group' is;*
- *describe how learners in a new class can become a 'real' group;*
- *present ways by which teachers can help the group formation process.*

In the Introduction we already mentioned that class groups are powerful social units and group characteristics considerably influence the rate of learning and the quality of time spent in class. In this chapter, we will first provide a more precise definition of what a 'group' is. Then, we start our exploration of the dynamics of class groups by going back to where everything starts: the first few lessons spent together. This is a highly important period in group life because much of what will happen later has its seeds in these first encounters. In describing how a group is formed, we will first examine the *initial emotions* characterising the first few classes, then go on to analyse a key component of the group's emerging internal structure, the *intermember relationship patterns*, and finally discuss practical ways to promote the gelling process of the class.

1.1 What is a 'group'?

What is a group? If we think about this question, it soon becomes clear that not every grouping of people is a 'real' group. For example, people sitting in an airport terminal waiting for their flight are not a group, and neither are the people in the reading room of the public library. So what makes a group a 'group'?

Human beings are group beings . . .

'People grow up in groups, sometimes called families; they work in groups, as engine crews, design teams or hunting parties; they learn in groups; they play in groups, in a multitude of team games; they

make decisions in groups, whether these be government commit-
tees, village councils or courtroom juries; and, of course, they also
fight in groups, as street gangs, revolutionary cadres and national
armies. In short, human beings are group beings.'

(Rupert Brown 2000:xv)

Rupert Brown (2000:3) has offered the following minimalist,
common-sense definition of groups: 'A group exists when two or more
people define themselves as members of it and when its existence is
recognised by at least one another.' In other words, a group qualifies as
a 'group' when it has become a psychological reality for insiders and
outsiders alike. We can, of course, try and provide a more detailed
and more descriptive definition. After reviewing the literature, Ehrman
and Dörnyei (1998:72) identified the following characteristic features of
a 'group':

1. There is some interaction among group members.
2. Group members perceive themselves as a distinct unit and demonstrate a level of commitment to it.
3. Group members share some purpose or goal for being together.
4. The group endures for a reasonable period of time (i.e. not only for
   minutes).
5. The group has developed some sort of a salient 'internal structure',
   which includes:
   > the regulation of entry and departure into/from the group;
   > rules and standards of behaviour for members;
   > relatively stable interpersonal relationship patterns and an estab-
   > lished status hierarchy;
   > some division of group roles.
6. Finally, as a direct consequence of the above points, the group is held
   accountable for its members' actions.

The question, then, is: Are language classes real 'groups' in the
psychological sense? They certainly are as they display all the above
features: class groups are characterised by considerable interaction
amongst the students; they are distinctly recognisable units with which
learners typically identify strongly; they have an official purpose; they
usually operate for months if not years; they are highly structured and a
student's good or bad achievement/behaviour usually reflects well/badly
on the other class members.

13

1.2 Initial emotions in class

> ***Think about it first***
>
> Imagine you are going to start learning a new language and the first
> class begins in just a few minutes at a new school. You don't know
> your classmates or your teacher. How do you feel and what are you
> thinking?

Let's start at the very beginning: the first lesson. Because we teachers
have had so many 'first lessons', it is easy to forget how stressful this
time might be for learners. It is comparable to walking into a party when
you hardly know anyone there. This is how a Hungarian university
student recalled in an interview how she first felt in a language course:

> *At the beginning, when I didn't know the group, I was always
> nervous – when nobody knows the others yet and doesn't even dare
> to approach and start getting to know them. Everybody is alone
> and so very shy; you don't know what you can joke about and
> what you can say to the others without offending them; you don't
> even know if they are good people or bad ones . . . It's all so
> uncertain. You don't know how other people's minds work.*
>
> (Ehrman and Dörnyei 1998:110–111)

This account is consistent with the research reports on how members
of any newly formed group feel (McCollom 1990). Indeed, if we think
about it, it is easy to understand why the process of group formation is
so difficult for many learners. Students must deal with others whom
they hardly know, and they are uncertain about whether they will like
them or, more importantly, whether they will be liked by them. They
observe each other suspiciously, sizing up one another and trying to find
a place in an unestablished and unstable hierarchy. They are on guard,
carefully monitoring their behaviour to avoid any embarrassing lapses
of social poise. They try to present ideal images to one another, while
hiding any signs of weakness. Those who lack sufficient social skills
often find this process very demanding and frustrating. But even for
socially adept people finding an identity in the group is no easy task.
The 'fusion with the group' requires redefining themselves and constructing identities as group members rather than separate individuals –
synchronising their behaviour with that of others by restricting it to
some extent without relinquishing their uniqueness as autonomous
human beings.

At the same time, learners also have doubts of a more academic
nature. They are uncertain about how much they will benefit from the

classes and they do not know what working in the group will entail and whether they will be able to cope with the requirements. Learners keep comparing themselves to others, many of whom appear to be more competent and proficient. Joachim Appel, a language teacher turned language student, had such thoughts as he listed his fears (Bailey, Curtis and Nunan 2001:110):

> *My fears: being called on to say something, mistakes, corrections, irony, ridicule. I keep comparing myself to the others. Even more important for my well-being than I thought: comprehension of what is said in class.*

Students are also striving to get used to the teacher's personality and style, and working out which behaviours are acceptable or desirable to the teacher. And, of course, all these complex processes are happening simultaneously while learners are also expected to do certain language tasks using the target language with others. A very stressful situation indeed!

The most common unpleasant feelings that many learners experience the first time they are in a new group are:

- general anxiety;
- uncertainty about being accepted;
- uncertainty about their own competence;
- general lack of confidence;
- inferiority;
- restricted identity and freedom;
- awkwardness;
- anxiety about using the L2;
- anxiety about not knowing what to do (comprehending).

Although the list is long, indicating that there is usually considerable emotional loading 'in the air', this may not be obvious to the onlooker, as on the surface the first language classes tend to run smoothly and harmoniously. In their search for approval and acceptance, learners are usually on their best behaviour and the social interaction between them often resembles polite 'cocktail party talk' (Yalom 1995). This is, however, no idle period in the group's life: scholars are in a general agreement that underneath the surface much structuring and internal organisation occurs, and within a very short time the group establishes a social structure – peer relations, status hierarchy, role and norm systems – that will prevail for a long time (cf. Ehrman and Dörnyei 1998; Forsyth 1999; Shaw 1981). It is up to the teachers how well they can utilise this initial smooth period to lay down the foundation of healthy future group development.

Questionnaire 1

How students feel in the first few lessons of a new class group

Thank you for filling this form out. You will learn about the group results in a few days.

*Please put an 'X' in the slot on the continuum which best describes how you **typically** feel in the first few lessons spent in a **new** class group (**not** this class).*

relaxed ___:___:___:___:___:___ nervous

confident ___:___:___:___:___:___ shy

sociable ___:___:___:___:___:___ withdrawn

willing to use the L2 ___:___:___:___:___:___ reluctant to use the L2

Now try and think back: how much has this class helped you to feel more . . .

relaxed?..

....

confident? ....

....

sociable? ....

....

willing to use the L2? ....

....

Is there anything you would suggest that we do to make the time spent in class more enjoyable and useful? ....

....

Questionnaire 1 offers a quick way of taking the 'emotional temperature' of the students in the forming period. The initial items are formulated in a way that they refer to general feelings rather than feelings towards the particular situation the learners are in – this way it may be easier for them to produce honest responses – and relating the general to their current experiences is a good conversation starter.

What about you, the teacher?

So far we have only mentioned that the beginning period is stressful for the learners. However, teachers are also members of the group and very often they also have anxieties of their own. You may be new to the school or may never have taught the particular L2 level before. You may be unfamiliar with the textbook or the type of course to be taught. You may be inexperienced or simply nervous in the company of new people. Even seasoned teachers often have 'stage fright', particularly during the group formation stage.

Indeed, from the point of view of emotional orientation, many teachers are not unlike the other members in their class groups. A great deal of the psychological processes underlying group formation apply to teachers as well. For this reason, it may be particularly important for you at this stage to take part in the classroom events as an 'ordinary' group member by joining – as much as is feasible – some of the ice-breaking activities and, in a reciprocal fashion, sharing some personal information about yourself with the students. Naturally, in your position as group leader and knowledge source, you also have unique tasks and concerns; these are discussed in Chapter 6 in more detail.

> *Reflection*
> Ask other teachers how much and what kind of information about themselves they initially share with their students. How do you feel when you hear personal information from a teacher or speaker?

1.3 Intermember relationships

> *Clearly explained . . .*
> 'The initial event in group interaction, the establishment of a relationship between two or more persons, is often referred to as *group formation*. It is evident, however, that the formation of a group is a continuous process. That is, the formation of the initial

> relationship is a necessary condition for group existence, but a group during its existence is in a never-ending process of change. The relationships among group members . . . are modified from day to day. The modifications are relatively large early in the life of the group; after the group has established quasi-stable relationships, the changes may be so slow and of such lesser magnitude as to be almost imperceptible.'
> (Marvin Shaw 1981:81)

The first aspect of the group structure that emerges during the group formation period is the pattern of newly formed *relationships* between the learners. Already after the first few encounters there will be instinctive *attractions* between some class members, whereas others may have taken a dislike towards some of their peers. According to Shaw (1981) and Schmuck and Schmuck (2001), initial attractions are caused by factors such as physical attractiveness; perceived ability and competence; similarities in attitudes, personality, hobbies, living conditions, and economic and family status (see Table 1). These factors, however, are usually of little importance for the group in the long run. A key tenet in group dynamics is that group development can result in strong cohesiveness among members *regardless of*, or even *in spite of*, the initial intermember likes and dislikes (Dörnyei and Malderez 1999; Rogers 1970; Turner 1984). In a 'healthy group', initial attraction bonds are gradually replaced by a deeper and steadier type of interpersonal relationship: *acceptance*.

The concept of 'acceptance' was highlighted by humanistic psychology in the 1950s, referring to a feeling towards another individual which is non-evaluative in nature, has nothing to do with likes and dislikes, but is rather an 'unconditional positive regard' (Rogers 1983) towards the individual, acknowledging that person as a complex human being with many (possibly conflicting) values and imperfections. As Rogers (1983) has put it, acceptance involves 'prizing of the learner as an imperfect human being with many feelings, many potentialities' (p. 124); it could be compared to how we may feel toward a relative, for example an aunt or an uncle, who has his or her shortcomings but whom we know well and is one of us.

One of the most important characteristics of a good group is the emergence of a general level of acceptance between members, and this will override even negative feelings between some. That is, we can actually come to accept group members even if we would perhaps dislike them as individuals outside the group. This surprising and seemingly unrealistic claim has received consistent support in the research literature (see, for example, Turner 1984) and we have also

Table 1 *Factors enhancing intermember attractions and acceptance*

Initial attractions:
- physical attractiveness
- perceived ability and competence
- attitude and personality similarities
- shared hobbies
- living near to one another
- similar living conditions and family status
- comparable economic status

Acceptance (later):
- learning about each other
- proximity (physical distance)
- contact
- interaction
- cooperation
- the rewarding nature of group experience and the successful completion of whole-group tasks
- extracurricular activities
- joint hardship
- common threat
- intergroup competition
- the teacher's role modelling

observed the power of acceptance in our own teaching practice. When this acceptance is modelled by the teacher, it becomes easier for students to do themselves.

1.4 How to promote acceptance

It is our experience that the teacher can play an important role in helping the class to gel by creating appropriate conditions and selecting suitable activities for the first few lessons. We must realise that peer affiliation does *not* necessarily occur automatically, which is attested to by the numerous language courses we have seen where after months spent together, students do not even know each other's names. The following account about an unsuccessful group by a young adult learner of English is by no means unique:

> *Well, this was a group of a rather 'disintegrating' kind. That is, it was the typical case when you have two 45-minute lessons a week, and you don't know the others attending the course at the beginning of the semester, sometimes you can't even recognise them by face, and neither do you know at the end of term who the people*

> *are with whom you have spent 14 times 90 minutes. And . . . the group did not really have any cohesiveness, didn't move into the same direction.*

So how can we consciously promote acceptance among our students? Here are a number of factors that will help bring the students together (cf. Dörnyei and Malderez 1997, 1999; Ehrman and Dörnyei 1998; Hadfield 1992; Johnson and Johnson 1995; see Table 1).

Learning about each other

By far the most crucial and general factor fostering intermember relationships is *learning about each other* as much as possible, which involves sharing genuine personal information. Acceptance simply does not occur without knowing the other person well enough. Enemy images or a lack of tolerance very often stem from insufficient information about the other party which, when left as it is, can grow into escalating 'cold war' tendencies and bullying. A great deal of this necessary learning about each other can actually be done in the target language, as part of a learning activity, thus serving the parallel purposes of helping the group to form and to learn the target language. Therefore, we would recommend that you periodically include low-risk self-disclosure activities to help classmates become more familiar with each other. Remember, the most interesting thing to talk about is yourself – forget the cardboard characters of Suzi in New York and Billy in London from the coursebook.

Rose Senior (2002) on information-gathering tasks – we couldn't agree more!

'In order to encourage the students in their classes to interact freely with one another, language teachers often devise tasks that require students to gather information from their peers. This information commonly relates to personal likes and dislikes, preferences, habits, hobbies, skills, experiences, and so on. I have seen teachers handle information-gathering tasks in widely differing ways. Some teachers consider that the task is finished when students have filled out their individual grids. In such cases the information-gathering task has a pedagogic purpose (to practise a new language form, such as "Have you ever . . . ?") but not a social one. Other teachers intuit the group-building potential of having plenary sessions in which the information gathered by individuals is tabulated and focused on by the class as a whole. This gives students the opportunity to learn

---

more about their classmates . . . Focusing on the content of what people say about themselves, rather than on the form alone, enables classes of language learners to evolve into learning communities, in which students know and respect one another as people.'

(pp. 401–402)

Proximity, contact and interaction

Proximity is the formal term used to indicate the physical distance between us. This is a powerful factor that can create some solidarity with the other party in itself – it explains, for example, the occasional feeling of commonality with others in a lift. This is why the seating pattern in the classroom is of special significance, and regularly moving people around in the first few classes is an effective intervention technique teachers can use to be in proximity with everybody else and to keep the class 'flexible' (see section 1.7 for practical tips on how to do this).

Contact refers to situations where learners can meet and communicate spontaneously – an obvious factor to promote relationships. Examples of high contact situations include the time spent in meeting places such as cafeterias or the various outings and other extracurricular activities the school organises. *Interaction* is more than contact; it refers to special contact situations in which the behaviour of each person influences the others. This interdependence is a powerful gelling agent. In the language classroom a great deal of interaction occurs, for example, when students have to do something together in small-group activities or in project work.

> ### From an interview with a student about a 'bad' group
>
> A: [In this group] students had few opportunities to get in close contact with each other.
> I: So what should the teacher do?
> A: For example, if the teacher could divide students into small groups to do some activities. They would get used to talking to each other. Without such activities students do not have the means to get to know each other. And then their relationship would naturally remain cold.　　(Adapted from Lin, 2002)

Cooperation

Cooperation between members for common goals, for example to accomplish small group tasks, helps them settle into cohesive groups.

Cooperation is, in fact, a type of interaction in which students are 'positively interdependent', which will result, according to Johnson and Johnson (1995), 'in an emotional bonding with collaborators liking each other, wanting to help each other succeed, and being committed to each other's well-being' (p. 19). Student collaboration can be successfully promoted by including certain tasks – such as role-play performances, problem solving activities, project work, filling in worksheets, and preparing group reports – in which students work towards a common goal and which require the preparation of a single 'group product' (see below).

The rewarding nature of group experience and the successful completion of whole-group tasks

The *rewarding nature* of group activities increases attraction toward group membership; the actual rewards may involve the joy of doing the activities, approval of the goals, success in achieving a goal (like completing a group task), and personal benefits (such as grades or prizes). Not surprisingly, groups are naturally more rewarding when they do well rather than fail; indeed, a history of success is an excellent gelling agent; for example, remarkable sporting achievements – say, the winning of a tournament by a local team – have been known to bring whole communities together. The successful completion of whole-group tasks is a particularly salient way of emphasising a sense of group achievement, and if there is a tangible group product (e.g. a poster or a newsletter) this will serve as an ongoing reminder of how effective the group can be when working together.

Whole-group activity: Group poem (adapted from Malderez and Bodóczky, 1999:48–49)

1. Ask the group to brainstorm adjectives they associate with 'our group'. Write these on the board and then ask them to vote on the best four.
2. Point to the first of the four adjectives and elicit new associations by asking: 'What else for you is . . . (adjective 1)?' These need to be more than one word; e.g. if someone offers 'a smile', ask the group to clarify: 'Whose smile?' or 'When?' Three or four phrases for each adjective are elicited and written on the board. Again, the participants vote for the one they like best for each adjective, and the 'others' are rubbed off.

---

3. Reveal then to the group that they have just created a poem about their group and read (present the similes in whatever order seems most poetic):

Our group is as (adjective 1) as (phrase chosen)
Our group is as (adjective 2) as (phrase chosen)
Our group is as (adjective 3) as (phrase chosen)
Our group is as (adjective 4) as (phrase chosen).

The result is typically interesting and often beautiful. You can put it on the wall or give copies to all the participants. Sometimes the words become a catchphrase for the group.

Extracurricular activities

There is something very powerful about extracurricular activities: one trip can 'make' the group for a number of reasons. First, such experiences are (or should be) typically stress-free and fun, resulting in a rewarding group experience. Second, during such outings students lower their 'school filter' and relate to each other as 'civilians' rather than 'students'. The experience will then prevail in their memory, adding a fresh and real feel to their school relationships. Add to this that extracurricular events usually offer a greater variety of positive roles for students to take than the rather restricted environment of the language classroom, and thus allow students to show themselves to the best of their abilities. Such outings can be exploited to the full by the group-sensitive teacher.

> **From an interview with a student**
>
> A: *Basically, the whole group got to know each other very well after the first two months.*
> I: *Did something particular happen?*
> A: *A day-trip. It was organised by a teacher and it went so well that the whole group became friends then.*
> (Adapted from Triantafyllopoulou 2002)

In recognition of its group-building function, some sort of extracurricular outing is often built into educational curricula. The most prominent example we have heard about is the South Korean practice of 'Membership Training', which involves students going on 2 or 3 day trips to special resorts that are usually maintained by educational authorities for such purposes.

Joint hardship and common threat

Strangely enough, there is a consensus in the literature about the beneficial group effects of *joint hardship* that group members have experienced, or will experience, for example by carrying out some tough physical task together or being in a common predicament. In such situations acceptance will be fostered by the joint effort to overcome the obstacles, and having coped with the hardship situation is an example of group achievement that often becomes an indelible element of the group's history.

A special case of joint hardship is the experience of some *common threat*, for example the feeling of fellowship before a difficult test or exam. Its positive role is due to the cooperative effort students make to reinforce each other, thus enhancing group attraction. Sometimes the common threat can become the teacher and playing tricks on the 'dreaded' teacher can become some of the group's best memories, as attested to by stories at reunion parties. Students also often stick up for their classmates against the teacher when they feel an injustice has occurred, as in the example below:

> I: *Why do you think this class was so special to you?*
> A: *We were supporting each other; we were close to each other.*
> I: *What do you mean by supporting each other? How?*
> A: *Some pupils had problems with the teachers.*
> I: *What kind of problems?*
> A: *Four pupils were sitting next to each other and were making noise, and fuss all the time. Thus, teachers made a decision to send two of them in other classes. The whole class decided to abstain from lessons for two days so as to prevent the placing of these pupils to different classes.*
> (Adapted from Triantafyllopoulou 2002)

Obviously, we do not advise enhancing group cohesion at this cost. Teachers can avoid becoming the common threat first of all by being fair and allowing students negotiation rights. In the case of common threats, an effective way for teachers to bond with their groups is to indicate clearly that they are on the students' side. This is what Tim did when he wrote the song 'Crazy TOEFL' (Murphey 1977) when teaching students who needed to pass the TOEFL to get into US universities. The song made fun of the test and built group unity.

Intergroup competition

Although earlier we emphasised the importance of cooperation, in certain circumstances competition can also be used to build friendship. In fact, competition can be a kind of collaboration when people unite in an effort to win. Individuals alone should not compete against each other, but rather small groups of individuals within the class, which is referred to as 'intergroup competition' (e.g. games in which groups compete within a class). During the process of supporting each other towards the common goal, group members build positive inter-dependence and empathy for each other. Therefore, in an in-class competition you may want to put students together who would not normally make friends easily, and mix up the subteams regularly. Once there have been several intergroup competitions within the class and students are in rapport, they may be ready to compete effectively as a whole-class group in school-wide competitions.

The teacher's role modelling

Friendly and supportive behaviour by the teacher is infectious and students are likely to follow suit. Flanders and Havumaki (reported by Schmuck and Schmuck 2001:125) conducted an experiment in an upper-elementary school to examine how teachers can influence the students' friendships with each other. The researchers asked a group of teachers to respond supportively only to selected students in their classes: for a week, teachers praised students seated only in odd-numbered seats. In other, control groups, praise was directed to the whole class. The results were striking: when all students were asked to list friends in their classes, students in the odd-numbered seats in the experimental classrooms received significantly more friendship choices than students in the even-numbered seats. In the control groups – as expected – there was no difference between students sitting in odd- and even-numbered seats. The message from this study is clear: our (i.e. the teacher's) relationship with each student is not merely a private matter but is being modelled by other students. This implies that if we can sense that some student has been rejected by the others, we can help the rejectee to gain some peer support by giving them an extra amount of encouragement and praise.

From an interview with a student

A: *The teacher was very serious and strict. I think that's the teacher's problem. He didn't know how to . . . You know, people can only talk to each other in a more relaxed atmosphere . . .*

I: *And did his behaviour have any influence on the relationship between your classmates and you?*

A: *Yes, of course. If the teacher is very cold, it will naturally influence the students' behaviour. Students cannot get in close contact with each other. They have few opportunities to form close relationships.* (Adapted from Lin 2002)

1.5 On the importance of knowing each other's names in class

All the factors/methods listed above have been used effectively to improve students' relationships with each other but there are three points that we believe are so important for classroom practice that they warrant a more detailed discussion: the importance of *knowing each other's names*, the use of *icebreakers* and the benefits of *moving students around* regularly. Let us start with names.

Interesting research

Tom Kenny (1994) once did some simple and yet profound research in Japan to find out whether remembering a student's name effects a student's performance. When he asked 150 college students about the significance of names, 89% of them said it was important for a teacher to remember student names. But 85% said that teachers did not usually remember their names and almost 20% believed that their names were not remembered by *any* of their teachers. To evaluate the effect of name-learning, Tom then compared the answers of the students whose names other teachers usually did not remember but he did (Group A), with the answers from the students who did not have their names remembered either by other teachers or by Tom (Group B). The difference between the two groups was shockingly marked: students in Group A reported that they found the class considerably more interesting: on a five-point scale (where 5 = 'my most interesting class' and 1 = 'my least interesting class') they had an average of 4.28, in contrast to 3.54 in Group B. Furthermore, Group A students reported speaking 'English only' more often in speaking tasks, enjoyed speaking English much more and, in accordance, evaluated their progress more highly. Finally, even more strikingly, the percentage of students who thought that their English had improved in the course was 80% in Group A and only 44% in Group B!

What's so important about names? There is certainly something special about them. Not knowing the others' names in the class has a far more serious consequence than most teachers would assume. We have found that in classes where we did not manage to learn the students' names we had trouble talking to them. Even to relate to them. A teacher knowing a student's name, and the student knowing that the teacher knows it, is extremely important for that student's constructed identity in that class. A student who even thinks the teacher does not know their name will often feel they are invisible in the group. Being anonymous is almost as if you do not exist in the group. And indeed, we fear, many students feel they do not exist in many classes all over the world where time is not taken to at least get to know each other's names. In our haste to get through the curriculum, the student is too often left behind, an insignificant number in a class, as Taiwanese teacher Chia-yao Lee noted in a graduate school action log to Tim in October 2002:

> *I didn't pay much attention to my students' names whenever I called someone (at random) to do the activity or to answer my question. I have to admit that there was something missing . . . I don't know how to describe this 'something' exactly. But it's just like I am talking to an 'it', but not to a human being when I don't know what his/her name is. Anyway, I tried to pay attention to my students' names, and memorise four or five names each time.*

Sample name-learning activity

True names and false reasons
Students sit in a circle. Student 1 says his or her name and a false reason about being in the class (e.g. 'I'm Otto and I'm here because I lost my way.'). Student 2, sitting next to Student 1, first repeats what Student 1 said then introduces him or herself and also adds a false reason. Student 3 repeats Students 1 and 2's statements before introducing himself or herself, etc. Variation: providing false reasons is usually a simple and effective way of generating a light-hearted atmosphere with lots of laughter. We have also used this task with other information, such as a false profession or skill; something you have never done; something you are proud of or own, etc.

> ### *How Tim gets students to learn each other's names*
>
> I semi-jokingly tell students '*We are going to have a test in a few days on everybody's name.*' Students introduce themselves briefly in a variety of activities and I ask pairs to test each other as they point to people and name them. I give them a class list so that they can practise visualising everybody's face with their name. For the first two or three classes I allow them a few minutes to test their partner again. The actual test a few days later is simply to have them look around the room and name everybody in their head. Then they write in their Action Logs (cf. section 8.1) how many they got, e.g. '18/25' and have to find out the names of those they don't yet know for a similar test in the next class. A test like this does not embarrass anyone because nothing is said out loud. I also demonstrate trying to memorise everyone's name in the first few classes and make a few mistakes and they see it is OK to make mistakes and ask people again what their name is. 'Sorry, what's your name again?' is a standard greeting in the first few classes for any new partner, even when they know their name.

As the research box above also illustrates, knowing names has a beneficial effect on the communicative classroom, but a similar positive impact is achieved by the fact that students can see you making an effort to learn their names. Kenny (1995) quotes the following passage from a learner's journal:

> *In the class on Friday, I was impressed because I found you are really trying to remember students' names. Not many teachers remember names as fast as you do and some of them don't even try. Maybe that's why your class is always fun!*

Thus, remembering students' names is a powerful rapport-building tool for the classroom. The Teaching and Learning Center at the University of Nebraska actually has a useful list of 22 tips and methods for teachers striving to learn their students' names: (http://www.unl.edu/teaching/Names.html). As they note, learning names does take some work, but the payoff is enormous (remember you *are* in Space 2!). Not only will student performance improve, but the teacher will be rewarded with smiles both in and out of the classroom. Let us note just a few examples:

- *Learn students' names – not just where they sit in the class.* Our brains have great associative place memories (Mary is behind Joe and

Sally in that corner). You may want your students to sit in the same seats for the first few classes to use that place memory. Then, get them to change seats and learn their face divorced from a place.

- *Photograph or videotape students.* You can look at the picture or tape and test yourself away from the classroom and just before you go to class.
- *Make students learn each other's names.* Get students to sit or stand in a circle and throw a crumpled ball of paper (or any object) around the circle, saying 'My name is . . .' each time they throw. Then tell them to throw it to someone without telling their name and the person who receives the ball has to thank them, using their name ('Thanks, Bill'). After the students have heard everybody's name, each student with the ball has to list the names of the two people sitting/ standing on their left and right.
- *Make students quiz you outside of class.* This one is the most fun. Tom Kenny tells his students that for homework, when they see him around campus in the next week, they have to walk up to him and ask, 'What's my name?' And he has to tell them. Of course, not every student asks him, but the ones who do have a lot of fun trying to 'stump the teacher'. If he can't say their name, he just keeps guessing! The humbling experience of making mistakes speeds up the learning process and shows students that teachers are not perfect.

From an interview with a student

I: *Could you tell me a bit more about the bad group?*

A: *To be honest, I can't remember the names of the people in it. I didn't know any of them . . . It was very hard to approach each other . . .*

I: *What was the cause of the group being bad?*

A: *I guess, communication . . . Lack of communication. That's the primary cause.* (Adapted from Usui 2002)

1.6 Icebreakers

How can we help our students (and ourselves) to get to know each other? A special category of classroom activity, *icebreakers*, can offer the answer. These were first introduced in L2 teachers' resource books in the late 1970s, specially designed to be used in the first couple of meetings of a newly formed group or when a large new intake joins the group. The purpose of these exercises, in Frank and Rinvolucri's (1991) words, is to get people to learn each other's names and become aware of each other as people. Well-chosen icebreakers help to relax people, get them to unfold their arms, to smile and to laugh . . . In doing these exercises people learn a little about other group members consciously and a vast amount unconsciously. (p. 9)

That is, icebreakers help to set members at ease. Collecting unconscious information about each other is especially important from the point of view of affiliation because learners identify with each other more easily when they see the others moving, hear their voices, talk to them, and establish personal relationships during the first few classes. With appropriate icebreakers, students and teacher may feel at home in class after the first few occasions, and treat each other as old acquaintances who have shared common experiences. In addition, these activities will also open up shy and withdrawn students, and help set informal norms concerning the desirability of being active, taking the initiative, having fun and becoming 'complete' human beings. Icebreakers make it difficult to merely act out mechanical student roles in superficially social classrooms.

Characteristics of good icebreakers (source: Ehrman and Dörnyei 1998:237)

Good icebreakers should:
- help students learn each other's names;
- ensure that everybody talks to everybody else, even if only briefly;
- involve sharing personal information;
- include various learning formats (e.g. pair-work, small group work, larger group work);
- allow students to try out various roles safely;
- promote cooperation;
- involve as much action as possible;
- move people around in the classroom;
- involve as much humour and fun as possible.

Good icebreakers should not:
- be embarrassing (e.g. by involving touching or disclosing too intimate information, or by putting people in the limelight before they are ready for it).

Sample icebreaker: find out about the others

Ask the students to write the first names of all their group mates on a piece of paper under each other, and then draw three columns next to them. In these they will collect certain information about everybody, preparing a sort of class chart. This may include personal information such as: How far away do you live? With how many people? What's the last book you've read? What are your favourite TV programmes and the ones you most dislike? A good way of rounding up the task is to interpret the charts, e.g. Who lives the farthest away? Which is the group's favourite TV programme?, etc.

1.7 Moving students round

Tim's students all do 'Action Logs', reporting after every class about the activities and how things went. He chooses certain student quotes to put in class newsletters anonymously for other students to consider (cf. section 8.1). In 2000, he placed the following comment from a student's action log in a class newsletter:

> I think changing partners every time is a really good idea because we can make friends!

In the next set of action logs nearly half the students commented in a similar way that it was great that they were making friends. He also gave a copy of that newsletter to his colleague, Brad Deacon, who also does action logging and newsletters. Brad returned the newsletter and had scribbled in the margin beside the above comment, 'It's amazing how many students say this [i.e. "making friends"] first instead of "learning" – or maybe it isn't amazing.'

Our 'language-teaching self' wants students to change partners often mainly to learn more from a variety of people and to be able to re-use language they are learning many times in a short span of time. This makes good pedagogic sense. However, what the many student comments like the one above show is that more important to students than learning is *making friends*. This of course happens as they interact and learn from each other, but when students proclaim, 'I love this class!' they don't really mean the subject but rather the fact that *they like themselves in the class because they have confirming friends.*

How to do it?

Having students change partners regularly with a lot of interaction and personal information sharing usually helps to form and deepen relationships and thus early acceptance. This can be done simply, for example by 'numbering students off' (two times 1 to 20 for a 40-student class) and they find and sit with their partner who has the same number. A variation is to ask the whole group to line up according to some criterion (e.g. birthday, number of minutes slept last night) after which they are counted off in groups in the order in which they now stand. For more advanced students, you may be able to tell them they need to sit with someone different every week.

Students report, as Kanako does below, that after a few weeks, they really like the routine of changing partners and that it helps to make friends:

> At first I didn't want to change partners. Now I have three new friends. I'm excited to come to class and have a new partner each week. I want to know everybody.

This mixing of students also reduces the power of cliques and integrates loners more quickly. Having an unknown partner provides a bit of facilitative anxiety and makes students pay more attention in class. Changing partners in the middle of class can stimulate them physically also after doing stuffed-in-a-chair seat-work for most of their classes.

1.8 Summary

In this chapter we have covered the following main points:

- The forming period in a new group's life is of special importance as very soon an internal group structure emerges that will prevail for a long time, affecting the group's future functioning.
- This group formation period is emotionally loaded for both the students and you, the teacher. The initial anxious emotions can be calmed and soothed through structuring non-threatening ways for getting to know each other.
- The most important initial elements of the group's structure is the emerging pattern of peer/intermember relationships. These relationships help to construct for the students a classroom identity and a sense of a learning community.

> *Something to remember . . .*
>
> While many teachers may attend to the questions 'Do you like this language? Do you like this class?', perhaps the more fundamental question for a *student* is 'Do I like myself in this class?'

- In order for a cohesive group to develop, the initial likes and dislikes should be replaced by acceptance among the students. The teacher can do a lot to facilitate this process, for example by using 'ice-breaking' activities and frequently moving students around. Engaging them in recursive activities in which students interact individually with many partners allows them to get to know many members of the group.
- Remarkably, students' names appear to be extremely important for triggering classroom identity construction, inclusion within the group and overall self-confidence.

> *Important questions about group formation*
> - How do you get to know your students' names and interests?
> - What methods do you use (could you use) to allow students to get to know everyone?
> - How could you get students to regularly interact with a variety of partners? Would they appreciate it?
> - What icebreakers have you used successfully? Which would you like to try?
> - How much do your tasks give students the opportunity to share genuine personal information?

2 Managing the class: Rules, norms and discipline

This chapter will:

- *describe the role of various rules and regulations in the group's life;*
- *present ways of developing a constructive system of classroom norms and 'learning contracts';*
- *discuss the implications of group norms to the broader question of classroom discipline.*

When people are together, in any function and context, they usually follow certain rules and routines that help to prevent chaos and help everybody to go about their business as effectively as possible. Take traffic, for example: if there didn't exist some rules, most of us wouldn't dare to sit in a car – of course, this is exactly why every country in the world has developed their own 'Highway Code'. But traffic is also a good example to illustrate that there is more to rules than simply whether they exist or not: Why is it that some of the traffic rules seem to be generally observed in a given context, whereas some others are constantly violated (e.g. we rarely jump the red light but often park illegally)? And why is it that cultures differ widely in the extent to which they observe certain rules and not others? Or, more generally, what makes a rule work? And are all rules as explicitly formulated as the Highway Code? In this chapter we will address these questions with regard to the classroom situation and examine how class rules contribute to the group's life and to the level of discipline in the class.

Even kids assume norms

With a small children's summer camp class in Switzerland once, I (Tim) had my seven students line up at the door at the end of the first class and answer a simple question before leaving. On the second day at the end of the class, I simply said 'goodbye,' but they all lined up at the door again waiting for my goodbye question before they would leave. They had assumed that lining up at the

---

door for a goodbye question was the 'norm' for this class and they thought we had to do it every day. And so we did.

2.1 What are 'group norms'?

Most teachers and students would agree on the need for certain 'rules of conduct' in the classroom to make joint learning possible. These implicit and explicit dos and don'ts that regulate the life of communities have been called *group norms* in group dynamics; as Oyster (2000:26) succinctly puts it, norms are 'the way things are done around here'. All groups have norms, consciously or not, and these concern at least two broad areas of public life:

- *social* (i.e. what the common values are and how we relate to each other);
- *procedural/task* (i.e. how we do things together).

Such norms influence all the details of group life, from the way of dressing and the volume of speech, to the amount of laughter and what taboo topics to avoid.

> *Yes!*
> 'If you think your behaviour isn't controlled by norms, think again.' (Carol Oyster 2000:27)

> *Think about it first*
> Take a moment to identify one or two groups you belong to. List what some of the norms that have to do with common values are. Then list some of the procedural norms for the group.

In educational settings we find many classroom norms that are explicitly imposed by the teacher or mandated by the school (e.g. in some countries students have to put their hand up if they want to say something or stand up when answering the teacher's question). As a teacher, you may have made it clear that attendance is required, that grades go down with late work, or that it is OK to ask questions at any time. Some teachers go so far as to give a special handout describing the kind of behaviour they want in the class and what is allowed and what is not allowed.

However, we need to realise also that the majority of the norms that govern our everyday life are not so explicitly formulated and yet they are there, implicitly. And if they are violated, everybody notices it. Many of these 'unofficial' norms seem to evolve spontaneously and unconsciously during the interactions of the group members, for example by copying certain behaviours of some influential member or the leader. These behaviours then become solidified into norms, and these 'unofficial' norms can actually be more powerful than their 'official' counterparts. Classroom norms regarding learning effort, efficiency and quality can considerably enhance or decrease students' academic achievement and work morale. For example, in many classrooms we come across the 'norm of mediocrity', which refers to the peer pressure put on students not to excel or else they will be called names such as 'boffin', 'geek', 'egghead', 'nerd', 'swot', 'brain', etc. (the list is endless). The question, then, is, 'How can we make sure that the norms in our classrooms promote rather than hinder learning?'

2.2 Group norms need to be discussed and willingly accepted

Real group norms are inherently social products. In order for a norm to be long-lasting and constructive, it needs to be explicitly discussed and accepted as right and proper. For norms to work, group members should 'internalise' them, to use Forsyth's words (1999), so that they become part of the group's total value system. This is true even with explicitly formulated school rules: even though students may obey them to a certain extent to avoid punishment or to appear agreeable, rules are unlikely to prevail for long unless they are willingly adopted by the majority of the members.

Quite so!

'Many teams simply ignore the notion of group norms. They assume that everyone knows how to behave in a group, so there is no need to take time to create explicit norms. It is not until a team starts to have problems that it becomes aware that team members are operating under different sets of norms.'   (Daniel Levi 2001:52)

In the light of these considerations, Dörnyei and Malderez (1997) have argued that it is beneficial to include an explicit *norm-building procedure* early in the group's life. They suggest formulating potential norms, justifying their purpose in order to enlist support for them, having them discussed by the whole group, and finally agreeing on a mutually accepted set of 'class rules', with the consequences for violating them also specified. Here are some suggestions and options for setting and communicating group norms/agreements:

- Provide students with a *written introduction* to you and your beliefs and how you foresee the class operating. Specifically, let them know how things might be different from what they are used to. For example, in Japan, many students have never had a class conducted all in English until they get to university. And most have never spoken a lot in classes. If the class is a conversation class, the teacher may explicitly announce that the course will be all in English. When writing your introduction, ask yourself, 'How will my class be different from what my students are used to?'
- List your *suggested norms* on the board or a handout and ask students to discuss them in pairs to see if they agree to them. They can also be asked to modify some or give additional ones. When a pair does question a proposed agreement or wants to add one, this is a good sign that they are investing themselves in the running of the class. Respect this. If they want to change something you feel is important, explain your point of view and why you think it is important for their learning. Still consider striking it from the list if they decide it is not appropriate. Their sense of participation and consensus-making is more important than you getting your way.
- After discussing and deciding on them, give *accepted class norms* out in writing. You can ask students to explain the agreements to each other once again, in the target language if they can.
- Put a list of class norms up for all to see, e.g. on a wall chart, to serve as a visible reminder of the rules the group has accepted (for sample sets of class rules, see the boxes below).
- *Point* to the list of class norms when talking about them.
- *Model* what you tell them. Walk your talk. If being on time is important and you aren't, the norm will not be taken seriously.

Sample set of class rules

Agreement

For the students:
- Let's be on time for class.
- Do your homework.
- Once a term you can 'pass', i.e. say that you haven't prepared.

- In small group work, help each other stay in the target language.
- When you miss a class, call a classmate and come prepared for the next class.

For the teacher:
- Let's finish on time.
- Homework and tests should be marked within a week.
- Give advance notice of a test.

For everybody:
- Let's listen to each other.
- Let's help each other.
- Let's accept each other and encourage each other.
- Let's not hurt each other or make fun of each other's weaknesses.
- It's good to take appropriate risks.
- It's OK to make mistakes.

Hook and Vass' (2000) minimalist set of class rules

'These are the three basic rules we have found to be most effective in our classrooms:

1. Follow your teacher's directions.
2. Keep your hands, feet and objects to yourself.
3. No swearing, name-calling, put-downs, etc.'   (p. 31)

Group norms that facilitate cooperative learner behaviour

- Be responsive to the needs of your group.
- Encourage others.
- Praise helpful actions and good ideas.
- Share your opinion with your peers.
- Take turns.
- Ask for help if you need it.
- Ask others for their ideas.
- Pay attention to and respect other people's opinions.
- Consult your team-mates before making a decision.
- Don't be impatient with the others.
- Be brief in discussions.
- Do not dominate.
- Make sure everybody participates.

(Madeline Ehrman and Zoltán Dörnyei 1998:264)

How can we change unproductive norms?

What shall we do if we notice that the class has evolved a norm that is counterproductive or damaging? Because of the social nature of group norms, here again we need to 'talk our way through' the problem. Wilson (2002:21) suggests that we take the following four steps:

1. First, we need to identify our concern. We can say something like, 'I'm worried that we've fallen into the habit of . . .'
2. Second, we need to get group members to discuss their perceptions and views of the issue so that everyone has a chance to become aware of the dysfunctional norm. A good starting sentence is, 'I'd like to know if the rest of you think there's a problem with . . .'
3. Third, we need to ask the group for an agreement to change the norm. For example, 'Well, we all agree that this is a problem. Can we discuss ways to act differently?'
4. Finally, after the group has identified a way to resolve the problem, restate the agreement: 'So we're agreed, then, that we'll . . .'

While changing unproductive norms will not necessarily go as smoothly as the four-step scenario above, discussing things openly will go a long way to building rapport with the group and understanding each other. The teacher might even learn sometimes that the students have a perfectly good reason for doing something that the teacher had thought was unproductive.

2.3 If one breaks the norms . . .

> *Makes you think . . .*
>
> 'In a course I teach on social psychology, I asked students, if they felt comfortable doing so, to identify a social norm and break it, then report the results to the class. One student, wearing a strapless, red sequinned, floor-length evening dress, went to the (only) mall in town, and simply walked from one end to the other. Did I mention the student was male? And quite hirsute (hairy). He was approached by security guards five times for simply walking the length of the mall. He had broken no rules, but people stopped and stared, and some called security officers!'   (Carol Oyster 2000:28)

What if someone breaks the norms? This is usually a great concern for novice teachers. However, with more experience, teachers often become aware that the more time they spend on explicitly setting the norms, negotiating them, explaining their value and modelling them, the fewer people go astray. And when they do, it is usually the group that brings them back in line. In her book on group work, Elisabeth Cohen (1994) summarises well the importance of a successfully developed norm system in educational settings:

> Much of the work that teachers usually do is taken care of by the students themselves; the group makes sure that everyone understands what to do; the group helps to keep everyone on task; group members assist one another. Instead of the teacher having to control everyone's behaviour, the students take charge of themselves and others. (p. 60)

Having the group on our side in coping with deviations and maintaining discipline is a major help. We should not underestimate the power of the class group. Students usually bring to bear considerable group pressure on errant members because 'Internalised norms produce not only the desired behaviour but a willingness to enforce rules within the group' (Cohen 1994:39). This can happen through a range of student behaviours, such as:

- showing active support for the teacher;
- indirectly expressing disapproval with shifts in eye contact, withdrawal from interaction with the offender;
- openly ridiculing or criticising the violator;
- putting the offender in 'social quarantine'.

Indeed, group pressure can be powerful enough to make certain students depressed, sometimes suicidal, and groups can also drive teachers crazy if they choose to. The following account by a language learner in an English as a foreign language course in Taiwan (adapted from Awane 2002) is a very good example of an internalised norm and how it ensures peer disapproval when it is violated:

> *The teacher emphasised an environment of 'No Chinese!'. Because Mandarin Chinese is our mother tongue, when we found we didn't know how to say something in English, we would speak Chinese. But the teacher told us not to speak Chinese in class. Over a period of time, this became a class rule. When you spoke Chinese, all the other classmates would say, 'No Chinese!'. Of course, there were some naughty children. They disobeyed the rule and kept speaking Chinese in class. Everyone could feel that they were bad; we would put a negative value on them and think they were children who disobeyed the rule. We felt in our hearts that their behaviour was not allowed and bad and wrong. We would still talk to them, but not very often indeed.*

> ## The power of the group: Harrist and Bradley (2002) on social exclusion
>
> '. . . peer rejection is one of the more serious problems in the schools today. Teachers, principals, parents, counsellors, and researchers hold this concern, but so do the children themselves. Even though only about 10 to 15% of children are consistently rejected by their peers, schoolchildren report worrying about peer relations as much or more than any other issue in their lives. Being excluded by school peers is a truly painful social and emotional experience. The pain of exclusion is evidenced by higher-than-average levels of loneliness and depression among rejected children.' (pp. 363–364)

Of course, we would want to avoid extreme ostracism by the group of any member for fear that it might be harmful. If the 'respect for individuals' is an actively modelled part of the norms, usually this can be avoided. Still, teachers need to be on the lookout for students who may be singled out, oversensitive and be receiving undue harassment from others.

2.4 How to maintain group norms in the long run

Having established effective group norms that are endorsed by the majority of the students is half the battle. The other half is maintaining and protecting these norms in the long run. The main principle of achieving this is straightforward: there should be regular reminders that these norms are important. The question, of course, is what the word 'reminder' can mean in classroom practice. Here are some ideas:

- *Wall chart:* Having the 'class rules' or 'class agreement' on display on a wall chart can serve as an effective visual reminder. We need to make sure that the chart is a prominent feature in the classroom and is not tucked away among other display items. The bigger and bolder, the better.
- *Teacher behaviour:* Learners are very sensitive to the teacher's attitude towards these norms; teachers as group leaders embody 'group conscience', and the model they set in their personal group behaviour plays a powerful role in shaping the class. The proverb 'Practice what you preach' is very relevant to group norms. Learners know when the teacher does not pay enough attention to having the established norms observed or when the teacher does not observe those agreements him or herself. These instances send a clear message

that the particular norms are not really important and, consequently, learners will rapidly discount and fail to follow them.

Indeed!

'Wittingly or unwittingly, the leader *always* shapes the norms of the group and must be aware of this function. The leader *cannot not influence norms*; virtually all of his or her early group behaviour is influential. Moreover, what one does not do is often as important as what one does do.'   (Irvin Yalom 1995:111)

- *Regular review of the norms:* Because groups never stay static but change and develop, the established system of classroom norms needs to be reviewed from time to time. This is particularly important if there are signs that the group is having problems with some norms; for example, there is conflict over the meaning or interpretation of the norm or the flouting of the norm becomes general.
- *Newsletters:* When students hand in regular reflections, as in 'action logging' (Murphey 1993; cf. section 8.1), they sometimes comment on the norms and these can be highlighted, anonymously, in newsletters for the whole class to model. For example, some of Tim's students made such comments as, 'Today, even after I left the classroom, my classmates and I still talked to each other in English' and 'I found if I played the role of a partner well, I could get more than I imagined.' The fact that these are students' comments probably makes them even more powerful communications in that students realise that they come from their peers who they will be interacting with in subsequent classes. The newsletters also present a view of what the whole class is thinking and doing so that other students are more in the 'know' and can follow suit.

Research finding

In the late 1980s, I (Zoltán) was teaching an adult evening language course in Budapest. Learners came from all sorts of walks of life and most of them studied the target language, English, beside their full-time job. No wonder, therefore, that they often found that the pressures of their work hindered their L2 learning. This was best reflected in the general level of completing homework assignments; these were compulsory in principle but the teachers in the school had no real leverage to bring to bear to enforce them. My estimate

---

at that time was that only about 60% of the assignments on average were done. That was the time when I first became familiar with the concept of group dynamics and decided to put the theory into practice. Therefore, in my group we agreed on the norm that learners should always prepare homework. I knew I had to give attention and group time to this norm; the theory suggested that if the teacher sometimes neglected to check the homework or was too lenient with those who failed to comply, this would convey a lack of respect for the norm. And then the homework-preparation frequency would gradually plummet. So I placed special emphasis on discussing and correcting homework and people who missed doing it were asked to make up for this. The results (Dörnyei 1995) were astounding: the overall completion rate of written homework exceeded 96%. And as I said above, this surprisingly successful outcome was purely the product of a principle of group dynamics in operation because I had no means whatsoever to discipline the 'naughty' students, some of whom were company directors, doctors and army officers.

2.5 Learning contracts

Teachers have for a long time successfully used *learning contracts*, which involve a formal agreement that is negotiated and ratified between teacher and students. The reason for preparing these contracts is usually the desire to motivate learners by setting specific learning goals for individual students (Dörnyei 2001b). However, contracts are not limited to individual students; the teacher might enter into an agreement with the whole class, in which case the contract will be similar to a formalised set of negotiated and accepted 'class rules'. Such contracts can vary in detail and elaborateness. They might describe a series of sub-goals that lead to a larger learning goal and the level of effort to go with these. Contracts may also contain specifications of the teaching method, the scheduling of various course components (e.g. tests, games, projects, etc.), the duties and responsibilities of both parties, and the reward or grade or other possible outcome. You may, for example, write down all the things that you feel you are prepared to give to the group, such as honesty, trust or experience (Hook and Vass 2000). Contracts may also detail agreement about what is to be done from the beginning to the end of a project or during a term, or after completing a specific section of the curriculum or course book. The following two examples present general, term-starting contracts from different classes taught by the same teacher, Péter Rádai, for English majors at Eötvös University, Budapest.

Example of a 'learning contract'

Contract

Between Ben Hur (pseudonym) and his 'English Teaching Methodology' group of autumn 1997 term:

- Both Ben and the group members are allowed to eat and drink during classes, and they can all make mistakes. Students also have a right to be tired and miss a few classes.
- Ben will do his best to create a good atmosphere. For this reason, he will respect his students and not be too strict with them. At the same time, group members agree to tolerate each other, be cooperative and participate in the activities.
- Students will do their home assignments. In return, Ben will finish the lessons on time. He will not be boring, and what is more, he is allowed to be funny.
- Let's help each other keep these agreements! Remind individuals when needed.

[signatures of every member]

Another example of a learning contract

Contract

We the undersigned have decided to keep the following rules:

	IS/ARE ALLOWED	MUST	MUSTN'T
BEN (teacher)	to make jokes to ask for feedback to give feedback on feedback to drink during lessons to start and stop activities	finish/start lesson on time be/come prepared provide a lot of activities understand students' problems	ignore anyone's opinion be/act offensive(ly) discriminate between group members force his will/views on the group
STUDENTS	to make jokes to miss some classes to refuse to give feedback to disagree with the teacher and each other to ask questions and ask for help to withdraw if they feel like it	turn up on time listen to each other do homework and come prepared attend lessons regularly	be late offend each other eat during lessons offend the teacher's feelings take advantage of the teacher's trust work against the group miss too many lessons

[signatures of every member]

2.6 How to deal with institutional and competing norms and rules

It is a very fortunate situation when it is entirely up to the teacher and the group to form the group's norm system. However, as we have said earlier, in most teaching contexts the school and, perhaps more importantly, the various educational authorities and boards impose a great deal of rules on classes. As Carl Rogers (1983:11–12) has formulated it,

> The schools are, to a degree never seen before, regulated from outside. State-designed curricula, federal and state laws, and bureaucratic regulations intrude on every classroom and every school activity. The teacher–student relationship is easily lost in a confusing web of rules, limits, and required 'objectives'.

The institutional rules coming from 'above' may clash with the teacher's own ideals or with what the group may think would work best for themselves. Even the best intentions and the most skilful teaching might be considerably less successful in an environment with many constraints. How shall we deal with this discrepancy?

In Chapter 5 we will discuss the impact of the physical and educational environment on the internal processes of the class group in more detail, and in the Conclusion we return to the question of how group dynamics can be extended beyond the classroom level. At this stage, we would like to emphasise the teacher's required sensitivity to synchronising the norm system of the class with that of the school organisation. On the one hand, we believe that it is the group processes in the classroom that have the most significant and direct bearing on student learning, and teachers *can* make a difference in any context. On the other hand, if there is a marked inconsistency between the school's 'hidden curriculum' and the classroom's environmental stimuli, the resulting dissonance can undermine some of the best efforts. This is why Schmuck and Schmuck (1997) argue that 'Attempts to improve classroom group processes often should be either accompanied or preceded by attempts to improve the organisational processes of the staff' (p. 248).

In concrete terms this means that during the initial 'norming phase' (for a description of group development in general, see the next chapter) it may be a good idea to raise the students' awareness of the relevance and importance of the potentially conflicting micro and macro levels of the normative climate. This can happen by discussing questions such as:

- Which are the main institutional norms?
- What is the rationale behind them?
- Why are they seen as necessary?
- How much do students agree with them?
- To what extent can they be adapted and adopted?

In addition, sharing ideas with colleagues, letting them know about your views and endeavours, discussing the conceivable gains and the possible difficulties, and thus developing a team of similar-minded fellow-teachers, may also be highly efficient in fostering a supportive social environment for the emergence of supportive classroom climates. In short, the processes you would like to promote among the students may work best if they are reflected by similar processes at the staff level.

2.7 Summary

In this chapter we have covered the following main points:

- Certain 'rules of conduct' are necessary in the classroom to make joint learning possible.
- Some of the classroom norms are explicitly imposed by the school or the teacher, but the majority of the norms that govern our everyday life are not so explicitly formulated.
- Real group norms are inherently social products and therefore in order for a norm to be long-lasting and constructive, it needs to be explicitly discussed and accepted as right and proper by the majority of the group.
- It is beneficial to include an explicit norm-building procedure early in the group's life.
- Unproductive norms need to be explicitly addressed and changed by consensus.
- If someone breaks a well-internalised class norm, you can usually count on the students to help you to enforce it.
- The proverb 'Practise what you preach' is very relevant to group norms.
- Class rules can be formalised into a 'learning contract' that is negotiated, ratified and signed by the whole class.
- There may be a conflict between your class norms and institutional norms, and the school's 'hidden curriculum' can undermine some of the best efforts; for this reason it is important to take time to bring the whole school staff on board or at least to 'sell' your ideas to a group of like-minded colleagues.

> *Important questions about norms:*
> - In your experience as a student, what memories do you have of different teachers setting up rules and structures (or not)? And how effective do you remember these being, or not?
> - As a student, what norms would you ideally like set at the beginning of a language course? Would these ideally change as the course progresses?

- What are some of your institutional norms that might hinder or interfere with the norming process in your classes? How do other teachers treat these norms?
- What are some of the national or regional directives in your teaching environment and to what extent might they help or harm the norming process in your own classes?

3 How groups develop

This chapter will:

- *describe how most groups develop through four stages;*
- *present insights into how teachers can facilitate this development.*

Think about it first

How conscious have you been in the past of groups going through different developmental stages? How might you label these stages? What stages are your present groups going through?

In Chapter 1, we talked about the initial stage of a group's life, discussing what is needed for a gathering of people to become a 'group' and how this new 'group' is more than the mere sum of all the members. Then, in Chapter 2, we saw how the emerging system of group norms, rules and agreements creates the conditions for effective functioning in a new group. The main message of this third chapter is that with the completion of the formation phase, our group-building work is not over. Groups do not stand still: they constantly develop in one way or another until the physical presence of the group ceases to exist. And one of the most important findings of the field of group dynamics is the recognition that this ongoing development follows certain general patterns that seem to 'cut across' different group types and contexts.

In this chapter we will look at these general patterns and consider how a familiarity with these can help us, teachers, to keep the learner group on the right track. In his most influential summary of group psychotherapy, Irvin Yalom (1995) concludes that in order for group leaders to be able to intervene in such a way as to allow the group to proceed, they must have a sense of favourable and of flawed development. We believe this is also true for language teachers: because the effectiveness of student learning is linked with group development (see

49

section 4.3, for more details), strategies to improve effectiveness should focus on helping teams reach the higher stages of development, and an awareness of the issues involved greatly promotes this process (Buzaglo & Wheelan 1999). Furthermore, knowledge of the principles of group development will also help to prevent teachers from feeling confused and anxious, particularly when things do not seem to go smoothly.

Indeed . . .

'The concept of group development is quite compelling. The idea that the group is more than the sum of its human parts and that groups move through predictable phases or stages is at once fascinating and a bit frightening.' (Susan Wheelan 1999:3)

3.1 Ehrman and Dörnyei's system of group development in learner groups

A great body of research in group dynamics suggests that groups move through similar stages during the course of development even in very diverse contexts. In a comprehensive review of the literature, Ehrman and Dörnyei (1998) concluded:

> The development of groups has similarities from one group to the next, making it possible to describe a group's evolution in terms of general phases, each with common patterns and themes. This generalizable change over time within groups has great practical implications for choosing appropriate inter-ventions, whether by a therapist or by a teacher. (p. 99)

At the same time, the authors also recognised that because of the typically rigid institutional constraints found in schools, certain group developmental phases become more or less featured in such contexts. In the end, they suggested that in classroom contexts it was particularly useful to distinguish four primary developmental stages:

1. Group formation.
2. Transition.
3. Performing.
4. Dissolution.

These are broad phases without any clearly demarcated boundaries but it is useful to discuss them separately because they represent very different concerns and priorities in the group's life. In Chapter 1 we have already looked at the first developmental phase, 'group formation', and in Chapter 2 we discussed one of its major components, the setting of norms. Thus, after a brief reiteration of the main issues involved in this initial phase, we will carry on the 'group story' where we left it in Chapter 1, at the point when the initial ice has been broken and the group has worked its way through the formation phase. In later chapters we will look at the specific phases in more depth (the conflicts associated with transition: Chapter 8; performing: Chapter 4; dissolution: Chapter 9). However, for now let us get a glimpse of the whole picture of their trajectory.

Well said . . .

'It is obvious that the course of a group over several months or years will be complex and, to a great degree, unpredictable. Nevertheless, mass forces operate in all groups to influence their course of development and to provide a crude but nonetheless useful schema of developmental phases.'   (Irvin Yalom 1995:293)

Group formation

As we saw in Chapter 1, the formation phase of group development is centred around getting to know each other and breaking the ice. The teacher's main role is to establish a friendly climate, manage group anxiety, clarify group goals and project enthusiasm for the group. Wheelan (1994) points out that this stage, more than any other, is characterised by significant member dependency on the designated leader. Members of a newly formed group find themselves in a new and not clearly defined or structured situation, and have therefore concerns about safety and inclusion. Politeness, tentativeness and deference to authority are typical features of group formation. Some work does occur at this early stage, but it is not up to the group's real potential and is typically initiated by the leader with the passive compliance of members.

Indeed . . .

'Forming a group is relatively easy: the initial stage of group life is usually harmonious as students get to know each other and begin to work together. Maintaining a cohesive group over a term or a year is far more difficult.'   (Jill Hadfield 1992:45)

The rugged transition

It is ironical that the developmental phase following group formation – labelled 'transition' – may not seem like an improvement in several respects. While the initial formation phase was usually orderly, with students doing their best to avoid any disruptions, during the subsequent transition phase members feel free to enter into arguments and debates. Peace is often replaced by conflicts and tensions, sometimes only brewing under the surface but at times erupting in a seemingly unexpected and illogical manner. This is not necessarily bad: but it has been found with groups of all kinds that they cannot start performing their main task effectively and harmoniously without going through this turbulent and rugged transition. In many ways, this is the time when the group has already come into existence but needs to sort out a few things about itself before settling into a daily routine. The group's main task at this stage is to make decisions about how it will operate and what roles members will assume in the process.

Thus, during the transition stage, differences and conflicts become common, stemming from disagreement and competition among members and between the group and the leader (see Chapter 8, for trouble-shooting tips). Because participants are becoming more familiar with each other and because some of their safety needs have been met, they will feel freer to express their individuality by becoming hostile towards one another and the task. What's more, as a counter-reaction to the all too prominent role of the teacher during the formation phase, the group is likely to seek to liberate itself from its dependence on the leader – conflicts between you and some students are almost inevitable. The main advice we would like to give you is 'Do not panic! Relax! Have patience!' It is at this storming stage that many good-willing teachers lose their confidence, blame themselves for their 'leniency' and, bitter at how the group that 'abused the wonderful opportunity they were given', resort to traditional authoritarian approaches to restore order. However, as Dörnyei and Malderez (1997) emphasise, the forewarned teacher will realise that this is a normal stage, welcome it as a sign of group development (much as L2 teachers welcome creative developmental language errors), expect some rain, and mediate and negotiate the group through the storm. In the end, the group is likely to be stronger for weathering the storm and they actually need it to make them come together.

We must note, though, that the transition phase does not have to be loaded with tension and conflict. The necessary component of this stage is not the 'fight' but the airing of dissenting views and possible alternatives. In groups that manage to gel particularly fast and in

---

Subgrouping

One process often observed in the early life of groups is *sub-grouping*. This refers to the natural human desire to form coalitions in the spirit of 'safety in numbers'. People in new groups are on the lookout for others with whom they share something in common and if they have found people with the same looks, interests, background, etc., they attach themselves to those. These emerging coalitions, then – as Oyster (2000:62) describes – 'may begin to manoeuvre themselves so that they can make a grab for power as the group develops'. Indeed, the first confrontational moves in the transition stage are usually made by such newly emerging formations rather than individuals.

---

which members have good communication skills, disagreements can be expressed and processed naturally, without strong emotional outbursts.

What happens if the group has successfully 'negotiated through the storm'? The idea is that the turbulent processes usually elicit counter-processes involving more discussion regarding goals, roles, rules and norms. We have found again and again that raising certain issues helps to eliminate tensions and once the storm has blown over, a new feeling of trust, supportiveness and commitment to the group emerge. Communication becomes more open and task-oriented and there will be an increased willingness to cooperate (Buzalgo and Wheelan 1999). Ehrman and Dörnyei (1998:129) summarise this as follows:

> Through airing and openly discussing bottled-up issues, through making (often negative) comments, and through the frequent use of 'ought tos' and 'shoulds', a new awareness of standards, shared values and mutual expectations may evolve and new rules/norms may be adopted. Thus the 'storming' and the 'norming' processes in classroom settings usually go hand in hand, and, if properly handled, can lead to the development of trust and an increased cohesiveness.

Most important group-building strategies to 'negotiate through the storm' in the transition stage

- Maintain the structure while providing space for the group to test its limits.
- Manage conflicts in a patient manner.

- Model expected behaviour, particularly with regard to respecting everyone's opinion.
- Clarify members' positions and summarise the main arguments.
- Pose a middle ground or acceptable alternatives.
- Praise members who are managing conflict well.
- Praise the group on its progress.

Performing

During the forming and transition phases, group members get to know each other and develop a sufficient foundation of trust for each other that will allow the group to start making decisions about the *division of labour* within the group. This is good news for productivity, since effective performance cannot take place without assigning specific tasks to specific people, and this process is oiled by mutual trust: Jack will only contribute his special skills fully if he trusts Jill to do the same. When this happens, we can start talking about the *performing group*, which involves the balanced, cohesive group in action, doing what it has been set up for.

The performing phase is a satisfying one: it is characterised by decreased emotionality and an increase in cooperation and task orientation. Having resolved many of the issues during the previous stages, the group has developed a more well-defined internal structure that includes agreement on norms, roles and decision-making procedures. The group has reached maturity, which enables it to perform as a unit and focus the majority of its energy on accomplishing desired goals. Although some work occurs during all the stages of group development, the quantity and quality of work increases significantly during this stage.

Of course, this phase is not total bliss either. It has long been recognised (e.g. by Shambaugh 1978) that the *emotional closeness* that makes the performing group so desirable regularly gives way to temporary *emotional distance*, forming a recurring, fluctuating pattern. That is, even with a mature group there will be good times and not so good times. However, the developmental level of the group is reflected in this cycle: as the group structure becomes more solid and members take on more and more responsibility for organising their work, the intensity of the emotional fluctuation decreases and affective energies tend to be channelled into the tasks. This stabilises task effort. We will come back to analysing how the cohesive group performs its tasks in the next chapter.

Dissolution

Finally, let us talk about the end of a group's life. An abrupt or unprepared ending of a group can leave a gap and can cast a shadow over the whole experience. It is a peculiar feature of humans that they spend a great deal of time looking back, evaluating what they have done and trying to draw lessons about how they should do things next time. In this way the past becomes closely tied to the future. A further – and even more peculiar – aspect of this self-analysis is that people's appraisal of their past performance does not only depend on the absolute level of success they have achieved but also on *how* they interpret their achievement. As Aldous Huxley has said, 'Experience is not what happens to a person, it is what a person does with what happens to him [or her]' – we dare say that this also applies to the whole group.

For these reasons, each group needs a leave-taking or *dissolution phase* that helps to consolidate what the group has accomplished and helps to erect bridges to the future. Members need to be allowed to feel good about their effort and to congratulate one another; reunion events need to be planned; loose ends need to be pulled together and unfinished business concluded. Last but not least, learners will also need guidelines and advice about how to maintain what they have learned or how to carry on improving their L2 competence. As Jill Hadfield (1992) has emphasised, it is important to give students some sense of continuity after the abrupt end of the course that may have been a major part of their lives for several months or years. Thus, for the group experience to be able to exert its full influence, the ending of a group needs to be managed just as deftly as the beginning (we will come back to this in Chapter 9).

Most important tasks for the teacher during the dissolution stage

- Prepare the group for the time outside the group.
- Permit and encourage expressions of feelings.
- Summarise and evaluate what the group has accomplished.
- Help to clarify future goals.
- Set up support networks and reunions.

3.2 When group development goes astray

It is generally assumed that in order to function effectively groups need to go through the four basic phases of development (i.e. formation, transition, performing and dissolution). However, this does not always happen and the group may bypass or never reach certain phases, thereby remaining a group of 'tourists' momentarily coming together to do individual tasks with little investment in relationships with others. It is important to talk about this because sometimes this incomplete development is due to the well-intended but misguided behaviour of the teacher/leader.

Skipping phases

Gerald Wilson (2002) argues that some group leaders can, in fact, guide their groups away from certain developmental functions. By 'getting straight to the point', a leader may in effect bypass the *formation phase* and steer the group straight into the turbulent transition phase without sufficient internal resources to cope with the conflicts. The following extract from a student interview about a French as a foreign language teacher (adapted from Triantafyllopoulou 2002) illustrates this well:

> *I remember the first time we saw her, she came in without introducing herself, absolutely nothing. She just started speaking French. From the very first moment on we didn't like her. Just imagine having a teacher for the first time, to come in the classroom and to start speaking French. It is terrible!*

We should note that the interviewee's problem in the extract did not really concern the exclusive use of the target language but rather the 'let's get down to business' attitude of the teacher, without offering any opportunities for introductions, icebreaking and group formation.

Other leaders may prefer reducing explicit conflict and arguments to the minimum, believing that there is something wrong with dissent. This, however, limits the *transition phase*, which is the road to consensus and autonomy; without looking at issues critically, the group may settle with inadequate, 'semi-cooked' norms and procedures, which in turn may backfire later on.

Regrettably . . .

'Trying to suppress disagreement is like trying to hold the lid on a pressure cooker. The more pressure that builds up, the bigger the explosion.' (Carol Oyster 2000:62)

Getting stuck

Skipping developmental phases can result in a group that makes unfounded progress that is not sustainable in the long run or in unresolved issues that surface sooner or later. An alternative worst-case scenario is the group that becomes *stalled*. Ehrman and Dörnyei (1998) point out that this scenario is particularly common in educational settings, because the traditional authoritative teacher role, the rigid curricula and the binding school regulations can impose powerful constraints that may prevent classes from working through the stages of development. For example, the class group may get bogged down in a never-ending yet never-resolved conflict stage, or group members may sit through the life of the group by basically remaining strangers (which is also common with seminar groups in higher education). One very common cause for getting stuck is the teacher's reluctance to loosen his or her grip over the students, which can stifle the performing phase (for more details, see Chapter 6).

When the group is unable to work through the phases of development . . .

'In one class, the group may not be able to "work through" the phases of development, and the interpersonal relationships may become cold and distant. Students will not become very well acquainted with one another in such classes because they are not communicating openly and personally. Indeed, some of the students will feel afraid to express their ideas; discussions, when they occur, will tend to be awkward and lack spontaneity. The students do not own the learning goals that the teacher presents to the students. Moreover, the rewards for conforming to classroom rules are extrinsic, and the direction of the group will be determined more and more by the evaluations of the teacher. The classroom organisation will, for the most part, become routinised, a narrow range of tolerable behaviour will characterise norms, and the teacher will be obliged to enforce classroom rules. Unfortunately, the picture represents the lion's share of public [state] school classrooms that we have observed during the past forty years.'

(Richard Schmuck and Patricia Schmuck 2001:65–66)

Individual differences within the group

The impetus of a group is such that usually most members are experiencing more or less the same things and going through the same group stages at the same time, like a school of fish navigating a stream. However, sometimes individuals will be out of sync with the rest of the group for various reasons and teachers might need to attend differentially to them. A new student who joins the class after a month will need some icebreaking attention and orientation while the others may already be in a transition stage. Even regular members may take more or less time in the different stages. Some students, for example, may remain in the transition stage for a good bit of time, trying to decide if they really want to be part of the group and adhere to the norms. In a healthy group, however, when such students feel that they are respected and allowed to work through this stage without being ostracised, they will eventually join the group more fully. In other groups, some students may not want the group to dissolve and may resist activities that try to bring closure to the group. So, although the main assumption in group dynamics is that a group displays an overall trajectory, some individuals may have their own unique trajectories. These individual trajectories do not necessarily require great attention on your part, but rather some patience, a general norm of tolerance and some time to let the group members help individuals adjust.

3.3 Summary

In this chapter we have covered the following main points:

- Because a group is in a continuous process of development, there is no point when we can stop our group-building efforts; without proper nurturing, even a healthy group may degenerate.
- Groups typically follow a trajectory of four developmental phases: group formation, transition, performing and dissolution. Although the phases overlap, they represent different concerns and priorities in the group's life.
- The teacher can do a lot to help students navigate these changes.
- Some individuals might not be aligned perfectly with the groups trajectory; however, with some patience they will eventually get there.
- Conflicts are an organic and necessary part of the transition phase and the most important advice to teachers about them is: do not panic. Relax. Have patience.
- Although some work occurs during all the stages of group development, the quantity and quality of work increases significantly during the performing stage.
- Even with a mature group we can find regular fluctuations of emotional distance and closeness amongst the members; however, the

more mature the group gets, the more the intensity of the fluctuation decreases and the more task effort stabilises.

- For the group experience to be able to exert its full influence, the ending of a group needs to be managed just as deftly as the beginning.
- Groups sometimes do not go through the four basic stages of development or reach the mature performing phase: they may skip a stage or get stuck.

> *Important questions about group development*
>
> - How do you remember yourself going through the four different stages in your own schooling (the first days of classes, the conflicts, the flow of good work, and saying goodbye)?
> - What is your experience of these stages in the classes you teach?
> - What stages do you recognise as being the most difficult for you to navigate with your classes? Why? How do you think you can improve them?
> - At which developmental stage are your current classes? Are any of them in danger of getting stuck?

4 The cohesive group: Relationships and achievement

This chapter will:

- *describe the characteristics of a mature group;*
- *examine the most important feature of a mature group: cohesiveness;*
- *present classroom techniques that promote group cohesiveness.*

> ### Think about it first
> 1. Remember a group in your past that worked really well and cohesively together. How did it work? What allowed the group to be so cohesive?
> 2. How cohesive are the groups you presently belong to and what makes them more or less so? What can you do to promote cohesiveness in these groups?

In this chapter we will look at the mature group that has developed internal cohesiveness and that has reached the 'performing stage' of group development. Obviously, if the group you teach has managed to come this far, that is very good news both for you and the students. But there are also some obvious questions to ask: How is group cohesiveness related to the *productivity* of the group? After all, just as the proof of the pudding is in the eating, our main interest in group dynamics lies in the assumption that a 'good' (i.e. cohesive) group offers a more supportive environment for learning than a group which has not reached the same level of maturity. A further question is whether cohesiveness can be 'overdone'. That is, can students be so friendly with each other that it may hinder their learning? Finally, are there any specific *techniques* we can apply to promote and maintain cohesiveness? This chapter will explore these issues and the 'performing stage' of group development in general. We want to look at this stage closely because it is the one we are trying to reach and maintain as long as possible.

4.1 The mature group

In Chapter 3 we described how group members first get to know and trust each other and then navigate the rugged transition stage, developing an internal structure for the group, before arriving at the performing stage. This is the point when we can start speaking about the emerging *mature group*, that is, a more or less balanced, cohesive group in action, doing what it has been set up for.

> ### Would that it could last forever . . .
>
> '[The performing stage] is very much like group nirvana. The group is now a mature group capable of extremely high quality work. Tension is very low. Trust is very high. Conflict is readily identified and effectively dealt with. Productivity is at its peak. The division of labour is based on skill and even the role of leader is transferred at different times to the individual in the group who can most effectively lead on a particular portion of the task. Would that this could last forever.'
> (Carol Oyster 2000:67)

So, what is the mature, performing group like? In a recent overview, Buzalgo and Wheelan (1999:113) have listed as many as 40 characteristics, the most important of which – from our perspective – can be summarised as follows:

- The group is highly cohesive, with a high level of intermember acceptance and cooperation.
- Subgroups are integrated into the group-as-a-whole.
- Periods of conflict can be frequent but brief and the group has effective conflict management strategies.
- Members are clear about and agree with group goals, and expect to be successful in achieving them.
- Members are clear about and accept their roles.
- The group norms encourage high performance and quality.
- The leadership style matches the group's developmental level, and is generally characterised by delegation or 'unleadership'.
- The group spends enough time discussing the problems and decisions it faces, and develops an open communication structure and participatory decision-making methods.
- The group has a defined work territory.

Some of these points are discussed in other chapters in detail. In the following we would like to address the first point in the list, which concerns what has historically been considered the most important group variable: *cohesiveness.*

4.2 What is cohesiveness?

In the latest edition of the *Handbook of Social Psychology*, Levine and Moreland (1998) point out that *cohesiveness* has been the subject of more research than any other aspect of group culture. This reflects the general belief of scholars that the closeness and 'we feeling' of a group is a key factor – if not *the* key factor – in determining every aspect of the group's life. But what exactly is this internal 'gelling force'?

Cohesiveness involves at least three components (Mullen and Copper 1994):

1. *Interpersonal attraction:* Desire to belong to the group because of liking the other members – this is, for example, often the primary source of cohesiveness of various clubs.
2. *Commitment to task:* Desire to belong to the group because of the interest in the task; in other words, the group feeling is created by the binding force of the group's purpose – this is often the primary source of cohesiveness in optional afternoon groups/circles at school such as the school choir or the drama group.
3. *Group pride:* Desire to belong to the group because of the prestige of its membership – this may be the primary source of cohesiveness in the school's football team that has won the county/state championship.

Although any one of the above components can make the group cohesive, in an ideal case two or three components are combined to create a solid basis of cohesiveness, resulting in a strong overall identification with the group.

Alas . . .

'Unfortunately, classroom groups often lack cohesiveness, especially when compared with other student groups, because common interest in the task, prestige and friendship are missing.'

(Richard Schmuck and Patricia Schmuck 2001:135)

Let's look more closely at the positive features of cohesive groups. Students in a cohesive group:

- Make each other welcome, show signs of mutual affection and provide active support to each other.

- Pay attention to one another.
- Remain in the group and convince others to join.
- Observe group norms and resist group disruption.
- Participate in group-activities willingly and are happy to cooperate with each other.
- Work easily with a variety of their peers, and therefore workgroups can be changed in a flexible manner.
- Actively participate in conversation and are ready to share personal details.
- Use 'we' and 'us' more frequently, and sometimes even develop a special jargon.
- Have more competitive relations with outsiders.
- Express more satisfaction with the group experience.
- Participate with each other in out-of-class activities (e.g. socialising or studying together).

It is very clear that some of the cohesive features above are parallel concerns in communicative language teaching (CLT), where recent emphasis has been on developing the students' communicative skills through participatory learning experiences in 'lifelike' communicative tasks. In effective CLT classrooms, teachers usually pay more attention to increasing the amount of communication amongst members, to enhancing the quality of the interaction, and to using various work-formations (e.g. pair-work, group work) which can be changed in a flexible manner according to the particular task. While many CLT teachers already attend somewhat to cohesiveness, we feel that CLT can further benefit from a more conscious and systematic approach to generating class cohesiveness.

Interesting research

Rose Senior (2002) has conducted a unique investigation in Australia: she followed the social development in eight intensive English language classes from the first to the final day of each course (which averaged ten weeks in length). The participants were adult learners from diverse cultural and linguistic backgrounds, and data were gathered through weekly classroom observations, extended weekly interviews with all the teachers, interviews with the students and open-ended questionnaires. The conclusion of her study fully supports a class group-sensitive teaching approach that fosters group cohesiveness:

'In this article I suggest that language learning is, by its very nature, a collective endeavour, and that learning takes place most effectively when language classes pull together as unified groups. I have shown that experienced language teachers set up learning tasks to accommodate not only the learning but also the social needs of their students. Such teachers, it seems, have an intuitive understanding of the fact that all language classes are composed of individuals who, with careful handling, can be melded into cohesive learning groups. The evidence suggests that skilful teachers regularly take steps to reinforce the feeling that everyone in the class is progressing along a collaborative language learning path, rather than learning in isolation from one another. It therefore seems that experienced teachers have adopted a *class-centred* approach to their teaching.'   (p. 402)

Measuring cohesiveness

In a study focusing on secondary school learners of English, Clément, Dörnyei and Noels (1994) used the following short questionnaire to measure the learners' perception of the cohesiveness of their learner group. Learners express the extent of their agreement with the six statements by ticking one of the boxes. The responses are then summed up by assigning a number to each category: strongly disagree = 1; disagree = 2 . . . strongly agree = 6. With negatively worded items (Items 2, 5 and 6) the scoring is reversed.

My group	Strongly disagree	Disagree	Slightly disagree	Partly agree	Agree	Strongly agree
1. Compared to other class groups like mine, I feel that my class group is better than most.	☐	☐	☐	☐	☐	☐
2. There are some cliques in this class group.	☐	☐	☐	☐	☐	☐
3. If I were to participate in another class group like this one, I would want it to include people who are very similar to the ones in this class group.	☐	☐	☐	☐	☐	☐
4. This class group is composed of people who fit together.	☐	☐	☐	☐	☐	☐
5. There are some people in this class group who do not really like each other.	☐	☐	☐	☐	☐	☐
6. I am dissatisfied with my class group.	☐	☐	☐	☐	☐	☐

Group cohesiveness is obviously a generally positive feature of a class but it is *not* synonymous with a blissful climate and unqualified comfort. Yalom (1995) points out that although cohesive groups may show greater acceptance, intimacy and understanding, they also allow greater expressions of conflict. Indeed, flare-ups are often tolerated in cohesive groups (perhaps because the group can afford to have them) as long as they are processed in a constructive way rather than leading to sustained hostility.

4.3 Group cohesiveness and group productivity/ effectiveness

A cohesive group has a more pleasant atmosphere than a non-cohesive class, but cohesiveness is not just about feeling good. Past research has consistently revealed a positive relationship between group cohesiveness and performance (cf. Ehrman and Dörnyei 1998). This is not surprising: in a cohesive group there is an obligation to the group, members feel a moral responsibility to contribute to group success, and the group's goal-oriented norms have a strong influence on the individual. The likelihood of 'social loafing' and 'free-riding' (i.e. doing very little actual work while still reaping the benefits of the team's performance) decreases in cohesive groups. Furthermore, members of cohesive groups actively support each other, which further increases productivity.

> *Indeed...*
>
> 'When what we are doing and who we are doing it with matter enough to us, we will work harder for our groups than we will ever do on our own.'   (Rupert Brown 2000:192)

We would like to draw attention to one crucial point in the previous paragraph: the importance of 'goal-oriented norms'. Cohesiveness does not automatically guarantee heightened productivity but only in cases when the existing group norms are *supportive* of production. In groups which are very close but are not interested in the 'official' purpose of the class we can have a situation whereby the group very effectively *refuses* to learn (and follows what have been called 'runaway norms'). And, given that cohesive groups have a firm structure and are therefore much more resistant to change than non-cohesive ones, if a cohesive group has anti-production norms, the teacher has a real problem. Thus, strangely enough, with regard to anti-production norms a group with *low* cohesiveness is better news for the teacher than a highly cohesive one, as students in the former are potentially more amenable to the teacher's influence (Schmuck and Schmuck 2001). We will come back to the possible downsides of cohesiveness later in this chapter (in section 4.5).

4.4 Promoting cohesiveness

Our discussion so far has hopefully made a convincing case for cohesiveness being a positive and sought-after feature of any learner group in general and language learner groups in particular. The question, then, is whether it is possible to cultivate it specifically. The good news is that there are a number of factors and conditions that considerably increase group cohesiveness, and many of these factors are at least partly under the teacher's control. Let us look at these factors and techniques one by one.

Well said . . .

'Despite the importance of individual friendship patterns and group cohesiveness, some teachers still maintain that they are employed primarily to teach content and that they should not be concerned about students' liking for each other or for the emotional closeness of the student group. We think such a view is shortsighted and naïve. It oversimplifies the social-psychological realities of teaching and ignores the psychodynamics that are integrally a part of most academic learning.'

(Richard Schmuck and Patricia Schmuck 2001:114)

Promoting acceptance amongst the students

Because 'interpersonal attraction' is one of the three main constituents of group cohesiveness, all the techniques that were discussed in Chapter 1 to promote intermember acceptance increase cohesiveness at the same time. These techniques included:

- learning about each other;
- promoting 'proximity' (physical distance), 'contact' and 'interaction' among the students;
- encouraging student cooperation;
- generating rewarding group experiences and organising extracurricular activities;

- coping with 'joint hardship' and 'common threats' together and participating in 'intergroup competition';
- modelling friendly and supportive behaviour by the teacher.

These factors, of course, can be combined to good effect. One highly popular cohesion-building activity that is used in many work places, the *outdoor experience programme*, is a good example of this (Levi 2001). In this activity, group members are presented with a series of challenges that they must deal with as a team. For example, they might have to cross a river using ropes, climb a mountain wall or do whitewater rafting. Such challenging activities certainly create proximity, contact and interaction; they require intensive cooperation; they are extra-curricular tasks and achieving them generates a rewarding group experience; furthermore, they qualify for 'joint hardship' and often involve some kind of intergroup competition. No wonder these outings are amongst the leaders' first choices when thinking of something that will bring people together.

Amount of time spent together and shared group history

We often find in relationships between two people that *the amount of time* the parties have known each other is a powerful factor to solidify and stabilise the relations. This is the same with groups: the 'Remember when we . . .' nostalgia usually acts as a strong glue bonding the group members together.

Group legend

A further important factor fostering cohesiveness is *group legends*. Jill Hadfield (1992) points out that successful groups often create a kind of 'group mythology', which includes giving the group a name and inventing special group characteristics (e.g. features of dress) in order to enhance the feeling of 'groupness'. Group members may also be encouraged to establish group rituals, create a semi-official group chronicle, prepare 'group objects' and symbols (such as flags or coats of arms) and find or create appropriate group mottoes and logos.

The class picture

Many students and teachers take pictures of the group at the end of their term together. We suggest doing it at the beginning of the course and giving copies to everyone for several reasons. It allows students to see their classmates out of class and helps them to

---

remember their names (it can even be an in-class activity when they are first handed out, 'Who is the guy with the red shirt next to the girl with a ponytail?'). Thus, it helps form a group. Ask them to paste the picture in the front of a notebook or textbook. Doing this is basically saying, 'You, and this group, are the course!' and lets them see each other, literally, more often.

Public commitment

Public commitment to the group also strengthens a sense of belonging, a fact that is well known, for example, to politicians and revolutionaries. Group agreements and contracts as to the rules are a kind of public commitment. Wearing school colours or T-shirts are another way of doing this.

Class newsletters for public commitment

Putting students' comments anonymously into class newsletters allows teachers to provide voices of commitment for all the class to consider and identify with. Tim included the following student comments in a class newsletter after spring break 2002, 'To tell the truth I really missed my friends here and I'm glad to see that they are still healthy and friendly like last semester.' Others wrote, 'It's the first time for me to speak so much English in class . . . Maybe it's because I had a good partner' and 'My partner is a hard-working student and a very responsible partner. She supported me to achieve 100% English today'.

Difficult admission

Another way to increase the cohesiveness of a group is to make admission into the group difficult. This is partly why exclusive club membership is usually valued very highly, and the same principle is intuitively acted upon in the various initiation ceremonies for societies, teams or military groups. Levine and Moreland (1998) report on research that has found that coal-mining crews, for example, use ritualised initiation ceremonies, in which newcomers are subjected to degrading and frightening experiences. These ceremonies serve several functions, such as testing how newcomers will respond to the dangers of coal mining, convincing newcomers that their safety depends on fellow miners and that the group has the means to punish nonconformity, and – last but not least – promoting a sense of solidarity within the group.

Investing in the group

It has been found that when members spend a considerable amount of time and effort contributing to the group goals, this will increase their commitment towards these goals and towards the group in general. In other words, psychological membership develops faster after some personal involvement in acts of actual membership, especially if publicly acknowledged. Therefore, eliciting some significant *investment* (e.g. completing a major project) early in the group's life may work towards group cohesiveness. The significant investment described in the following student newsletter comment concerns extensive reading:

> *It's incredible that most of the people are going to achieve their goals of extensive reading! Wow . . . That is such a great job. Through reading newsletters, I can see others' determination and strong will to expand their learning clearly. I also tell myself to keep up with them and I think this is a challenge for me to make my own world larger.*

Defining the group against another

Emphasising the discrimination between 'us' and 'them' is a powerful but obviously dangerous aspect of cohesiveness. It is amazing, for example, how effectively the rivalry between classes (e.g. in sports tournaments) can unite people within each class. There is a delicate balance to achieve here: while we would be very strongly against stirring up emotions against an outgroup in order to strengthen ingroup ties, it might be OK to occasionally allow students to reflect on how special their class and the time they spend together might be, relative to other groups. Note, for example, the following student newsletter quote:

> *In last week's Newsletter, I found that classmates usually share [about] our class with their friends in other schools. It's great. I did that before, [and] my friend told me that he wants to exchange classes with me. One of the reasons is that I can read newsletters as pleasure reading . . .*

4.5 Is there a possible downside to cohesiveness?

So far we have mainly talked about the bright side of cohesiveness. But is there a hidden dark side? It depends on our perspective: cohesiveness is usually positive from the relational point of view, but strong peer bonds do not always support the group's official goal and, thus, learning productivity. Let us briefly cover three potential problem sources: (a) cohesiveness unaccompanied by strong group-oriented norms, (b) 'groupthink' and (c) cohesive groups competing for time.

Cohesiveness without strong goal-oriented norms

Wilson (2002) points out that it *is* possible for a task group to be too cohesive. In such cases members begin to enjoy one another's company so much that they focus on their relationships rather than on their task. Soon the group becomes a *social group* and productivity will fall. This is, in fact, exactly what happened to Zoltán in a successful (and apparently too successful) adult English language course (Dörnyei 2001b:60):

> *This course was in many ways a most inspiring and successful experience: the group bonded well, the group spirit soared high, there was hardly any student attrition, and we generally had a good time. There was only one 'slight' problem: with the growing maturity of the group there was less and less actual learning taking place in the class. I spent long hours with a psychologist friend, who was at the same time a learner in this group, trying to figure out what was going on. The answer we eventually came up with was that some time during the course of the programme the group shifted its main goal: because personal relations within the group were becoming so very rewarding, social rather than academic goals became the group's main concern. To be fair, this made perfect sense from their point of view: after all, it is difficult to find fault with the argument that with regard to the members' general well-being, to belong to an accepting and supportive community and to acquire a group of new friends is not at all less important than mastering the English language . . .*

To show that this problem is not restricted to adult evening classes, let us present another personal account, by a Greek student (adapted from Koui 2002):

> *It was in the third and last class of junior high school, when I was 14. It was really nice because there was a bond among us, we were very close with each other. Our productivity was very low but the jokes and our silliness were childish and fun. Even the teachers laughed with us sometimes. We were innocent.*

Thus, too much cohesiveness without any firm goal commitment may move the group from its designated task to socialising, or cause a group to think less critically about its task. However, the reason for sharing these accounts is not to dissuade anybody from trying to promote group cohesiveness (and the vast majority of class groups – regrettably – remain so far away from this 'dangerous' level of cohesiveness that there is no need to worry). Instead, these examples highlight the importance of a strong, goal-oriented productivity norm in the class that accompanies cohesiveness (see Chapter 2, for a detailed discussion). Without this goal-oriented productivity, the group may even go to the other extreme and 'cohesiveness may support concerted and spirited anti-adult behaviour, as in delinquent gangs or defiant classroom subgroups or violent cliques' (Schmuck and Schmuck 2001:115). Oyster (2000) shares a similar concern when she talks about 'runaway norms', which refer to norms that violate the norms of the larger environment.

'Groupthink'

Another potential problem that may arise from a group being too cohesive is that students can value cohesiveness and their relationships with each other so much that they go out of their way to avoid conflict and are, thus, unwilling to challenge one another's ideas. As a consequence, they may let ideas about which they have reservations pass unchallenged, which of course might result in an inferior end product. Furthermore, out of respect for each other's opinions, group members may reject outgroup members who might disagree. We agree that stifling dissent and disagreements in such a way is a possible danger and, in fact, the phenomenon has been studied extensively by social psychologists under the label of *groupthink*.

Groupthink is evident when group loyalty undermines critical thinking, that is when in order to preserve a sense of cohesiveness and belonging, members not only suppress their objections but may even reach the point where they are unaware of any objections. That is, groupthink refers to situations in which 'groups take leave of reason' (Wilson 2002:253). The result is that members of the group endorse positions considerably more extreme than the average of their opinions as individuals, and group members reject out of hand any different views or evidence coming from outside the group.

How do we prevent the development of groupthink? Based on a review of the literature, Oyster (2000) suggests three possible courses of action to create an open, critical and grounded group:

- Outsiders should be brought into the group on a regular basis in order to keep the group in touch with outside norms and allow for the expression of divergent opinions.
- Group members should be actively encouraged to think critically; for example, whenever someone presents an idea, he or she may also be asked to mention some possible drawbacks associated with the idea. Alternatively, a group member can be assigned the role of the 'devil's advocate', that is, his or her briefing should be to actively find faults with whatever is being suggested to the group.
- The group leader should not express an opinion before all the other members have expressed their own, thereby avoiding the possible undue influence of authority.

Cohesive groups competing for time

One further example of how cohesiveness can get in the way is when students join extracurricular clubs which then place hard-to-achieve time demands on their members. This is seen often in first year university students' need for belonging. When students begin university, often far from home, they can feel very lonely at first until they have been accepted into a group. Often they join extracurricular clubs and groups that can become much more important to them for social reasons than their classes. Sometimes, especially in Japan, students will belong to one main club that requires a certain number of practices and meetings each week that build cohesiveness for their purposes but which can distract from or interfere with the students' academic goals. Students in such situations sometimes feel they are being disloyal to their new club mates if they are asked to spend more time on their studies. It is a time-management and a group-loyalty dilemma that many find troubling. If there is no cohesiveness and friendliness among members in the students' academic settings, the extracurricular groups will garner most of their time, and grades usually suffer. However, when students feel a part of a class and responsible to each other, they will usually find ways to manage their time. Teachers can help by explicitly explaining these things in class so that students can make more informed choices and plan their time better.

4.6 Summary

In this chapter we have covered the following main points:

- Cohesiveness is one of the most important attributes of a group: if it's there, everything else is likely to be OK, whereas a lack of it indicates some major obstacles in the way of group development.

- Cohesiveness forms a good foundation upon which groups can become productive: successful groups are usually cohesive.
- There are many techniques available to promote group cohesiveness; some of these have already been discussed in Chapter 1 when looking into the promotion of intermember acceptance.
- Group life has two aspects: socialisation and goal-oriented behaviour, the first supporting and complementing the second. However, some groups may cohere and permit socialisation to be their main task to the detriment of goal-oriented behaviour.
- Respect for the group and its members should not lead to uncritical groupthink.

Please bear this in mind . . .

'Despite a teacher's best efforts, there are always classes that fail to bond. Teachers should not feel guilty or inadequate when this happens. There are clearly a wide range of contributory factors beyond the teacher's control which can either enhance or inhibit the bonding process, ranging from the nationality mix of the students in the class to the size and location of the classroom. It is hoped, however, that . . . a general understanding of the principles of group dynamics can help teachers to develop a range of tactics which will enable their language classes to become more fully bonded.' (Rose Senior 1997:10)

Important questions about group cohesiveness

- Which classes and groups do you remember being particularly cohesive when you were a student? What made them so?
- Are you currently a member of any cohesive groups (in your professional or personal life)? What holds each group together (activities, beliefs, attitudes, common mission, etc.)?
- What do you do to create cohesiveness in your classrooms?
- What techniques would you like to try out to help you make a more cohesive class?

5 The classroom environment's contribution to group dynamics

This chapter will:

- *describe the nature and the impact of the classroom environment;*
- *discuss possible variations of the seating arrangement;*
- *consider temperature, lighting, decoration and music;*
- *present ways to increase student ownership of the classroom.*

> **Think about it first**
>
> How would you describe to a friend or colleague the way you arrange the environment of your classroom? What features would you highlight? What would someone see, hear and feel that was different about your classroom?

In sociolinguistics it is a well-established fact that the social situation exerts an impact on the communication that takes place in it. For instance, the same two people talking about the same topic would tend to use different language in a pub or at a royal reception. Similarly, groups do not operate in a vacuum: the setting that the group occupies (i.e. the actual classroom) profoundly influences the ways in which members behave toward one another. Levine and Moreland (1998), for example, report that groups working in dangerous, impoverished or confining environments (such as coal miners, submariners or astronauts) develop particular forms of interaction suited to the conditions they face (e.g. in order to take coordinated action and reduce conflicts among members). Thus, in these cases there is a clear interplay between the environment and the dynamics within it. Physical environments, however, do not have to be harsh or dangerous to affect group life; various more subtle aspects of the setting – such as floor space, lighting, temperature and noise – can also affect the operation in a dramatic manner. This chapter is about these effects.

5.1 The classroom environment

While the physical characteristics of the environment do not completely determine how effective teaching is, they can be major inhibiting or contributing factors (as any teacher assigned to the 'room from hell' can attest to). Most classrooms were not designed after paradise, but there are ways to make them more suitable for learning, even in the worst situations. In Japan's hot May, Tim actually ended up bringing his own rotating fan into his classroom to the great pleasure of his students. He made sure to make the white board attractive with drawings and colour when possible. He had students sometimes close their eyes and take mental trips to favourite 'cool' places and then return and describe them to their partners. He played environmental-sounds cassettes to empower their imaging over the blandness of the walls. When we use our creativity and remain flexible, there are ways to make the physical environment more comfortable for learning. Moreover, students usually recognise and appreciate these small efforts. Simply bringing a small plant to the class can change things, for you and your students.

Tim's post-Hawaii 'environment-shock'

I once went to a workshop at a nice hotel on the coast of the big island of Hawaii. The chairs were welcoming, the views from the windows were of 'paradise', it was quiet with sounds of the sea and sea birds, the temperature agreeable, even the island smells were pleasant. Just being so comfortable in such an environment allowed me to really focus my attention on the topic and learn a lot. When I returned to my classes at a large Japanese university, I was in 'environment shock'. They didn't turn on the heat in my classrooms until December, nor the air conditioning until June so we froze for the month of November and baked in May. There were some rooms with no windows and it was forbidden to hang things on the walls (which might distract students from another teacher's content). The old chairs and desks were too small for full-size adults and they crammed as many people as possible into the small rooms (really getting smelly in summer, sometimes). As with most new teachers, I had no choice of classrooms and had to take what they gave me. Teachers teaching in late afternoon close to the sports field also had to compete with the yelling of sports teams and cheerleaders. While at the seminar in Hawaii we had made a nice friendly circle with the 15 people; in my sardine-packed classes of 50 students we had to turn sideways to shuffle down rows to seats

---

in the back of the room or to distribute handouts. The physical environmental cards seemed stacked against me.

At the same time, let us beware of blaming the environment too much. Even in environmental paradise there are some groups that do not seem able to focus on learning and do not come together effectively. The ideal environment will not save a teacher with insufficient group development and teaching skills. And the inverse is also true: teachers will be able to overcome many physically debilitating characteristics with good skills and enthusiasm. One of Zoltán's best ever seminar groups actually met in a classroom that was so small and crowded that the door could not be opened (inwards) when everybody sat down . . .

Many teachers teach as if the physical environment were either unimportant or simply beyond their control and thus ignore the possibilities for change. The perception that major physical alteration is impossible in most school settings may actually be true, but if over-generalised it keeps teachers from at least changing what they actually *can* change. There are three other reasons why teachers so often fail to grasp the possibility of changing the physical environment:

1. The most traditional way of teaching involves the teacher facing the learners who are sitting in columns and rows, dependent on the authoritative teacher at the centre of the communication network; and through the teachers' own 'apprenticeship of observation' (i.e. years spent as students), they naturally feel that this is the right way a class should be organised with no need for any change.
2. When one teaches in this traditional way, it is so restrictive in itself that variables such as room size, the distance between rows, or décor do not appear to change the interaction pattern significantly.
3. Teachers often do not realise that they have a privileged spatial position in the classroom: they can see everybody and they may also move around to face whoever they want to talk to, and this leads them to assume similar comfort on the part of the students.

We contend that for all classes in general, and specifically for language classrooms, the principal mediational means of learning for any group is the *interaction* between the members. This flow of interaction is not only the basis upon which friendships are founded and grow, but it is also the main means of constructing learning collaboratively. This interaction can be helped or hurt by environmental factors. Naïve optimists, however, sometimes believe that they can override obviously unfavourable environmental conditions, and then are surprised if an event or class goes badly in an oversized room that they have not adjusted to, or if a meeting accomplishes little in a noisy restaurant. Below, we discuss the impact of size, temperature, lighting, noise and furniture arrangement. We ask how they may inhibit communication or how we might lessen and alleviate some of their negative impact by transforming the environment to make it more conducive to learning and group development. More subtle effects arise from our inherent human tendency to be territorial on the ownership of the classroom.

5.2 Spatial organisation

The flow of interaction and communication is greatly influenced by the spatial organisation in which we operate daily. While teachers may have little choice as to the shape of the room, the available furniture and the size and location of the windows, they do usually have more options concerning the arrangement of the desks and chairs (let us, for the moment, try and forget about all those benches bolted to the floor . . .). Taking advantage of these options can have potentially powerful effects.

The placement of chairs and desks exerts significant influences upon the status of the students occupying them, the patterns of participation, various leadership opportunities and the affective potential of group members. There does not seem to be one ideal seating arrangement; rather, seating arrangements serve particular work needs and should be purposefully matched with the type of interaction anticipated or encouraged in particular tasks (see section 5.3, for details). A creative teacher can use various arrangements to suite the activities that they are planning.

Tim's conference presentation in a huge room

I was once assigned to a huge room at an international conference. It was big enough for about two full-size basketball courts. The only door in it was right behind where the speaker's podium was and there were long heavy tables with chairs facing the front covering the front half of the room. The back half was empty (ready for a basketball game I mused to myself). I was there early and since there were only a few people present at the end of a long day, I wanted it to be more friendly and informal. I grabbed a chair and took it to the far end of the empty half of the hall. As people came in, I invited them to bring their chairs to form a circle with me in the back half. By the time it was supposed to begin, we had about 20 people in a circle for the last session of the day and we felt pretty cosy. However, suddenly another 40 people showed up who had got lost in the immense convention centre. Because we had lots of space, the circle simply expanded and within a few minutes we had a *huge* friendly circle. It felt wonderful to me to be able to see everyone in a group that size, and for everyone to be able to see each other. For the three or four interactive things we did I simply asked them to find a new partner each time to their right or left or to come to the centre and find someone. The centre was a wonderfully natural interaction space. Whenever I was talking I felt very comfortable simply sitting like everyone else. It was a magical presentation for me. The material I had was well prepared, but it was made immensely better by getting out of the constraints of the environment that keep people from seeing each other and moving around. I realised later that I also did not have to worry about latecomers interrupting the session from just behind where I was speaking. The whole thing was not planned or calculated, I simply took a risk based on my desire to be closer to a small group. It was amazing that the large group that I concluded with acted like a small group principally because they were arranged in a circle and could interact with many different partners in free movement in a short time.

Although we often may have difficulty saying why, we tend to agree about what room feels 'good' or 'bad'. Teachers know from experience that the space available for the group affects relationships. That, for example, a small group sitting in the back of a room while we teach in the front is uncomfortable. Experienced teachers will either ask students to come sit up front or walk toward the back to teach, taking control somewhat of the environment by bringing people closer together. And if just a few students are scattered in a large room, we ask them to sit together.

Tip 1

One way to get a scattered group of people together in a large room is to number them off with partners and then ask them to sit together near the front and tell each other something, for example about themselves.

Distance between the participants determines the feeling of intimacy. Too much space will usually be perceived as impersonal and can cause psychological distance and the feeling of insignificance, emptiness, isolation and anxiety (MacLennan and Dies 1992). Teachers who wish to create a friendly, positive environment in classes will arrange things so that people are close enough to interact and make friends. Research studies suggest that highly cohesive groups occupy smaller spaces than non-cohesive groups (see Forsyth 1999). On the other hand, if there is too little space, members may feel crowded and confined and avoid interaction. They might even become violent as they compete for more space.

Spatial organisation and member status

There is a relationship between *status* and *spatial position* in groups. Occupants of certain positions are accorded higher status than occupants of less favoured positions. There is, for example, a well-established 'head of the table effect': the person sitting at the head of the table, or in the middle of the side with the fewest seats, is attributed high status, probably because it is associated with the leader's position – leaders prefer this place because it has the greatest visual centrality, so they can maintain a greater amount of eye contact with the other members and can comment more frequently. Thus, simply by being in the centre of the communication network, the person at the head of the table can exercise a greater amount of interpersonal influence. On the other hand, as Oyster (2000) reports, the person seated at the leader's direct right may have the lowest positional power at the table as this is where the secretary is traditionally located in some cultures. Oyster's point, however, also shows how culture-dependent such spatial stereotypes can be because in some other cultural contexts sitting at the right hand of a powerful person is a highly privileged position (e.g. we learn from the Bible that Jesus Christ sits at the right hand of God in heaven).

Students sitting in more conspicuous places in the classroom are on the receiving end of more attention and interaction, and thus are likely to get more involved in the learning process. In contrast, as Schmuck and Schmuck (2001) argue, a marginal seating position can give rise to feelings of being peripheral and unimportant, leading to a reduction of communication with others. In a sensitive account of various locational zones in large Pakistani classes, Shamim (1996) confirms this observation. She found in L2 classrooms that the majority of students experienced sitting in the back of the classroom as very demoralising. Furthermore, Lambert (1994) cites research evidence that seating position also has the potential for affecting teacher judgements about students, independent of their individual characteristics.

5.3 The arrangement of the furniture

The above discussion indicated that spatial issues affect the dynamics of the class group. While architecturally, teachers are limited as to how much they can change and adjust their classrooms, they are usually free to change the environment significantly through arranging the furniture. Whether it be setting up workspaces for small groups, corridors of access between chairs and desks, or innovating arrangements in novel ways, teachers need to realise how much they can really change and take control of more of their environments. We discuss some of the more common classroom seating patterns below as well as the issue of how to still be interactive when the furniture cannot be changed.

Traditional teacher-fronted seating structure

The most traditional spatial arrangement involves columns and rows of desks and chairs with the students facing the teacher. It is appropriate if communication is planned only between the leader and the group members (e.g. at formal presentations). It has been found to be very effective if the goal is to make sure that students pay attention to the presenter or perform independent seat-work without disruptions – after all, this arrangement does not offer any environmental support for peer interaction.

From the perspective of group dynamics, there are two main disadvantages of this spatial structure:

- It creates inequality among students: as we have seen above, differences in classroom locations are associated with different status, and this is projected to the students occupying these positions.
- The teacher-fronted arrangement is extremely controlling, emphasising only teacher–student visual contact and thus helping the teacher completely occupy the centre of the communication network. This enforced teacher-dependency is an obstacle to group processes.

> *Douglas Brown's recommendation to language teachers:*
>
> 'You may have had the experience of walking into a classroom and finding the movable desks all lined up in columns (not rows) that are perpendicular to the front wall of the room. Neat and orderly, right? Wrong. If you won't get fired from your teaching post by doing so, change the pattern immediately! Students are members of a team and should be able to see one another, to talk to one another

> . . . and not made to feel like they just walked into a military formation.'   (Brown 1994:412)

To have or not to have desks

Some teachers prefer doing away with desks altogether. Not having desks that separate people from one another can sometimes create a feeling of closeness and enhance interpersonal communication. At the same time, desks can also be seen as the students' 'private territories', where they keep everything they consider necessary for their studies. Thus, at first they may feel vulnerable without the safety of their desks and resist letting them go. It is also not easy to write on knees, and a modern communicative classroom will be concerned with process writing, interactive writing, poster-making and project-work. In accordance with our suggestion that seating arrangements may depend flexibly on the activity, it is nice to have the option to have desks or not, depending on the tasks you want to do.

Semi-circular seating structure

Probably the most common arrangement for small groups is a *semi-circular seating arrangement*, with the teacher sitting in the middle of the open end of the U-shape. This arrangement allows students to have direct visual contact with each other to increase communication, but still reinforces the leader's status because of his or her being in the centre of the communicative network. Whenever there is no 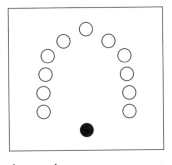 particular need to draw special attention to the teacher, you may want to close the circle to increase the self-organising ability of the group.

Circular seating structure

This arrangement has no predetermined leadership position as it physically *includes* the teacher in the group, equalising influences. A further advantage of sitting in a circle is that it fosters interpersonal attraction and involvement: Ehrman and Dörnyei (1998) report on studies that have found that people sitting in circle groups rated each other as more friendly than in other arrangements, and that the circular arrangement resulted in shorter pauses in conversation. However, just

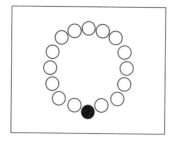

as suddenly not having your desk can present one with anxiety, sitting in a circle when you are not used to it can be intimidating as well. Some investigations have found that imposed intimacy can also be associated with negative feelings of confinement.

It is easy to believe that the circle is the ultimate solution to 'spatial equality'. However, several studies have shown that people seated opposite each other interact with each other more than people who are seated side-by-side. This means, that usually students in directly facing seats to the teacher will participate more than members sitting on either side. That is, positions in a circle are not always equal in their communicative 'status' and, therefore, it may be worth moving students and yourself around from time to time even if they sit in a circle.

Ad hoc clusters of chairs/desks

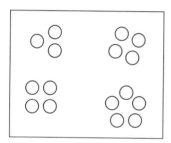

For building student autonomy and responsibility, tasks that call for a seemingly ad hoc positioning of the furniture in small groups of chairs/desks, such as games and small-group activities, are particularly useful. The big advantage of this spatial arrangement is that the teacher is not present in the students' primary communication networks. Such small-group activities, role-play performances, drama techniques, etc. require space and movable furniture – something which is unfortunately too often not available in the L2 classroom.

Tim observes Aiko's classroom

One of my responsibilities in Japan for a decade was going to see student-teachers from my university do practice teaching in local high schools. As would happen practically anywhere in the world, the student-teachers would inevitably teach just like the teachers they had been observing at the high school – in fact, they would feel obliged to. Desks were always in columns and students mostly silent, with perhaps a bit of choral repetition and a few students called on to answer questions. When I went to observe, there would usually be the regular teacher and perhaps an administrator or two in the back observing as well. Almost without fail, the teachers in the back and I would begin to nod off somewhere during the 50-minute lesson. We teachers in the back, more than the students, were not used to sitting without doing much and found it intolerably boring to just listen to a teacher talking. (Why this experience never changed the practices of the teachers in the back is a mystery . . .)

One time, this did not happen. There were five teachers sitting in the back observing and a few minutes into the class the student-teacher dared to ask students to move their desks together in pairs for an activity and then in fours. It was amazingly simple actually. Because the student-teacher was walking around monitoring their activities, the other teachers and I got up and began doing the same and we listened in on probably the most lively high school class we had ever seen. Everyone, students and teachers, agreed it had been a wonderful class, although the conservatives were concerned about the noise level and whether students were actually on task and if they were learning each other's bad pronunciation. I was ecstatic for the student-teacher and the potential for change in the system.

5.4 Temperature, light and decoration

Extreme temperatures can cause irritability, and reduced productivity, especially if the room is overheated. Forsyth (1999) notes that extremes in temperature can keep people from being friendly and seeking affiliation and thus works against groups uniting. We have heard that some prisons are kept overheated on purpose to keep the prisoners lethargic and with less energy to be violent.

In addition, dark and dull colours and poor lighting can depress the mood of the group (MacLennan and Dies 1992). While teachers cannot usually change the colours of the walls, they can open windows and turn on lights when this helps. At the other extreme, hyper bright neon lights can also be a nuisance. If natural light is available, we prefer using it.

Finally, the aesthetic conditions of the classroom are not to be ignored either. Pleasant decoration is not merely the icing on the cake but has been found to play an important role in facilitating learning. Wilson (2002) reports a study by Maslow and Mints from the 1960s, in which the researchers asked people to conduct the same task in three different settings: an ugly room (like a janitor's closet), an average room (a professor's office) and a beautiful room (a living room with nice furniture). The task involved rating various photos and – no surprise there – subjects gave more positive ratings of the photos, enjoyed the task more and wanted to stay with the task longer in the beautiful room. This recognition has been utilised, for example, in the language teaching method 'suggestopedia', where a pleasant classroom atmosphere is a central component of the method (cf. Larsen-Freeman 2000).

5.5 The ownership of the classroom

We humans, like many animals, are territorial by nature. Students who sit in the same seat in two consecutive classes are already apt to think of that place as theirs. As any new student who comes to a class can attest, you must be careful not to 'take' someone's usual seat as other students might say, 'You can't sit there. That's Mary's seat'. Having students move around in class, changing seats and partners from the very first day, not only keeps them from claiming a permanent position in the classroom and even feeling stuck there, but it can also allow them to get comfortable being anywhere in the classroom and thus claiming the whole room as theirs to a certain extent.

Students (just like other people) like to personalise their 'living spaces' by leaving their mark on the surroundings or furniture. Studies (see Forsyth 1999) suggest that people feel more comfortable, 'at home' and more satisfied with their work and interpersonal relations if they are allowed to mark their environment in their own way, much like office workers who put up pictures and plants around their cubicles. Teachers can also do this by the objects and music they might bring to class. Flowers, soft drinks and snacks can also help create a more humane, relaxed atmosphere.

'Territorialising' the classroom means that students are exercising increased control over their environment, which in turn can lead to more autonomous learning. To enhance group development, a teacher can encourage students to 'take over' control of the board, walls, furniture arrangement, etc., potentially adding to their maturity and autonomy.

5.6 Movement in the classroom

We have seen that a student's position relative to the teacher affects their feelings of involvement and participation. That is why we feel it is important when possible for the teacher to equalise things. This can be done in two ways: by the teacher changing positions in the classroom or by having the students change seats and positions regularly.

The teacher on the move

Teachers who walk around the classroom while talking to the class and teaching provoke a noticeable effect on students. When the teacher is near, heads go up and the students' attention increases. This can be caused by fear when students are unfamiliar with the teacher, or the teacher is considered threatening in the minds of students. However, increased proximity can also simply be a stimulation of difference and can cause a comfortable increase in intimacy and familiarity. Stimulating those in the back with a few minutes of your time is not a difficult thing to do. Try it. Just walk to the back of your room for part of your presentation of a new chapter or exercise. Or even try sitting down in the back next to a student. As John Fanselow says, 'Try the opposite!' And see what happens! We believe that a teacher's moving around the room provides more equal access to more students, more equal 'proximity time' – time to be close to students so that they become inspired to learn, rather than being distant and unaffected.

Students on the move

Another important variable in the furniture arrangement is the students themselves. Not only can we arrange the chairs and desks in different places, but we can also ask students to change seats and to be seated in a variety of group formations (see also section 1.7). Fixed position preferences, which often set in during the first few classes, can lead to the emergence of rigid, fossilised patterns of 'private spaces' that can negatively affect contact and interaction among students (see Chapter 1). The fixed seating also leads to subgroups and cliques forming and to potential conflicts among students and groups who are not familiar with each other.

Tip 2

An effective communicative activity that is centred around changing partners involves students working in pairs, discussing something. They then move around and summarise the information they have gathered or the conclusion they have come to, to another person assigned to them. Finally they return to their first partner and give feedback on the second discussion. If they do this as a

---

routine in several classes, students can learn that they must understand the messages they are receiving in order to communicate them to another, and more negotiation and meaningful communication takes place.

From a Vygotskian constructivist point of view, learning happens *intermentally* first, between minds in interaction, and only later becomes one's own learning, *intramentally*. With this point in mind we would want students to create intermental communications with as many other students as possible so that they could learn as much as possible. Working alone or always with the same partners can be boring. When students know they will be working with different partners every day, there is a certain facilitative anxiety that is created, a newness, and a stimulation that can bring the class together more as a group. Thus, we suggest to teachers that they consider having students change partners often for pair and group work in order to allow the participants to get to know everyone better and to learn from more perspectives, and also in order to keep the class lively and moving.

Loud and distant partners

Assigning students partners who are several seats away and instructing them that they have to talk to each other from their present positions has several advantages. Firstly, students have to talk louder and enunciate to be heard and understood over all the voices. Secondly, students overhear each other easily and thus they stay in the target language collectively, and they can also borrow language from their neighbours. Thirdly, it is a lot of fun.

5.7 Songs and music in the environment

Dull environments can be greatly stimulated with some appropriate music. 'Appropriate' music depends on the students' and teacher's tastes. Obviously, soft background music will soothe and comfort while louder popular music might energise students – thus, the choice depends on your need. When the environment is populated by musical anchors that students respond to positively, they are much more likely to buy into the activities with willingness and motivation.

General musical recommendations are:

1. No music when the teacher is talking.
2. Soft music at the beginning of pair or group work, stopped when the teacher wants to call back the attention to the front of the room.
3. Louder and faster music later in the class to energise students and sustain them.
4. A good rocker for goodbye when they are leaving the class, and also perhaps when they come in.
5. Very soft classical music for reading or solitary seat-work.
6. Do experiment and see what your students want and enjoy. Ask them to loan you presently popular songs and listen to them and see if there are songs you can use.

5.8 The ideal classroom?

When Tim was an MA student studying language teaching methodology, some of his fellow students were ex-peace corps people who had just returned from abroad. One named Rick had just come back from Africa. He kept asking professors who were lecturing how he could have done the things they recommended in his previous contexts where there were no pencils and paper, no blackboards, and rarely even any desks and chairs. Later when he started teaching at the university's English Language Institute as a teaching assistant, he stopped complaining and said something that really surprised everyone:

I used to think I was in the worst possible classroom situation in Africa. Most of the time we had no classrooms to speak of really. But now after teaching back here in these university classrooms I find it even more difficult. Here we usually only have pictures of animals and trees. Back there, I taught under a big tree most of the time and we would walk around for our lessons and talk about what real people were doing, what we were seeing. Life was our classroom. We were not restricted by four walls, a textbook, and grades. And it was so easy to teach. The community was our classroom.

Rick made many of us question our conventional thinking. Have we unnecessarily restricted ourselves by confining ourselves to the 'academic' idea of a classroom and learning? Many of us explored and found ways to expand our concept of the classroom by bringing the real world to the classroom and taking our classes out into the world. We took our students on short field trips around the campus for different language-learning activities, we held classes sitting under trees in the campus gardens, we invited a variety of guests to join our classes, some teachers even brought their children to the class.

Getting out of the box

TIM: In Japan and Taiwan, I have regularly taken my classes outside because it is simply more comfortable there, or I need more room (for juggling, a blind walk or 'walk-talks' – see below), and students seem more stimulated and alert when they are outside. It is also nice to show them that they can speak their target languages outside the classroom. Escaping from your classroom also allows you and your students to understand that you can learn anywhere and any time.

Going outside does require a certain discipline among the students and good places that are reasonably quiet need to be found. Outside will also be putting your class before the public eye and you may even have passers-by asking to join your class.

Probably the most common structure for outside classes is sitting in a circle in the grass. However, sitting on the grass is not always possible if it is wet or full of insects. I often do 'walk-talks' in which students in pairs arrange themselves in a circle around me. I give them a topic to discuss in a timed conversation and they walk around in the circle and talk. I stop them after a few minutes and ask the inside people to move one (or two or three) people forward to a new partner and tell their new partner what their last partner said and then re-ask the questions. I have also asked students to take a walk anywhere and be back in five minutes, walking and talking as they get on with a certain task.

The point is that we are not restricted by our classrooms. We have the world to teach in. Now that is a big physical environment to contend with.

5.9 Summary

In this chapter we have covered the following main points:

- There is a strong interplay between the physical environment and the dynamics in it.

- Components of the environment (what we see, hear and feel) are always to a certain extent adaptable by the participants. This offers a potentially powerful tool for teachers to use according to the group's needs.
- Some of the features that are often available for change to enhance learning are:
  where students are located;
  the variety of partners they interact with;
  how often they change partners;
  the placement of the chairs (U-shape, circle, etc.);
  the classroom temperature and lighting;
  the décor;
  the feeling of ownership of the classroom;
  the movement of the teacher and students;
  the use of songs and music;
  leaving the classroom and going outside.

Important questions about the impact of the environment on the group

- What are the most important environmental concerns for you?
- What kind of environmental problems do you feel you can change and how?
- What components of the environment can you do nothing about (and are you sure you can't)?
- What kind of music or songs might you choose to use?
- Have you ever taken a class outside? If so, how did it work?

---

6 The teacher as group leader

This chapter will:

- *provide a brief overview of the theory of leadership;*
- *in the light of the theory, discuss the functions of a 'facilitator-teacher';*
- *describe some basic characteristics of effective leadership styles in classroom contexts;*
- *address the issues involved in promoting learner autonomy.*

Think about it first

Remember a teacher you had who was a good leader in your opinion. What are the features that made him or her effective? What kind of a leader would you like to be as a teacher?

We will start this chapter by describing four classic theories of leadership, from various branches of psychology. These will provide clear evidence that *leadership matters*. They will also demonstrate that the optimal leader behaviour depends on the maturity level of the group – this means that a particular leadership style might be ideal in a certain situation but detrimental in another. In this chapter we will look into this relationship and try to outline the characteristics of the effective 'facilitator'.

How very true . . .

'Leadership is the fabled elixir. It can turn failing schools into centres of excellence. It is the potion that enables head teachers to inspire competent teachers into becoming masters of their profession. It is the process by which you allow your students to become winners.'   (Peter Hook and Andy Vass 2000:5)

6.1 Lewin and his colleagues' three leadership styles

Let us start our investigation of leadership characteristics by describing one of the most influential ever studies in social psychology, conducted over 60 years ago by Kurt Lewin and his colleagues (Lewin, Lippitt and White 1939). Working with American children in a summer camp, the researchers were interested to find out how the participants would react to three very different group leadership styles:

- *Autocratic* (or 'authoritarian') *leadership*, which maintains complete control over the group.
- *Democratic leadership*, where the leader tries to share some of the leadership functions with the members by involving them in decision-making about their own functioning.
- *Laissez-faire leadership*, where the teacher performs very little leadership behaviour at all.

The results were astounding, with the three groups showing highly significant differences from each other both in their productivity and their social relationships. Of the three leadership types the laissez-faire style produced the least desirable outcomes: the psychological absence of the leader retarded the process of forming a group structure, consequently the children under this condition were disorganised and frustrated, experienced the most stress, and produced very little work. Autocratic groups were found to be more productive (i.e. spent more time on work) than democratic groups, but the quality of the products in the democratic groups was judged superior. In addition, it was also observed that whenever the leader left the room, the autocratic groups stopped working whereas the democratic groups carried on. From a group-perspective, the most interesting results of the study concerned the comparison of interpersonal relations and group climate in the democratic and autocratic groups. In these respects democratic groups exceeded autocratic groups: they were characterised by friendlier communication, more group-orientedness, and better member–leader relationships, whereas the level of hostility displayed by the children in their relationships with each other in the autocratic groups was thirty (!) times as great as in democratic groups.

These pioneering results have been reproduced by a great number of studies over the past 50 years, and there is a general agreement that the evidence is consistent and clear in support of democratic, participatory leadership. Schmuck and Schmuck (2001) argue convincingly that autocratic class groups are often unable to 'work through' the stages of group development and, as a result, frequently 'get stuck' and become stagnant (cf. also section 3.2). In such cases, interpersonal relationships become formalised, distant and fragmented, dominated by cliques and subgroups rather than overall cohesiveness based on peer acceptance, and the group's learning goals and goal-oriented norms are not shared by the students. In a recent meta-analysis of past studies, Foels, Driskell, Mullen and Salas (2000) conclude that people in groups tend not to prefer to be 'subjected to domineering or manipulative leadership but instead are more satisfied when they are allowed to participate in group decisions' (p. 692). However, we must be cautious about equating 'democratic' with 'good': 'democratic' leadership refers to a style, and we can find both effective and ineffective teachers following this style; similarly, some 'autocratic' teachers can be better than others.

Nevertheless, Shaw's (1981) claim that it is much *easier* to be a good autocratic leader than to be a good democratic leader is noteworthy. Indeed, it is relatively simple and undemanding to be directive and issue orders, but rather difficult to utilise effectively the abilities of group members. This also implies, if we turn this claim around, that uninspired and unambitious teachers are likely to opt for an autocratic style since a tighter control over the students may result in a smoother course immediately and better results in the short term – and requires less effort! Is this why an autocratic approach still tends to dominate worldwide?

Have you?

'You may remember being given some advice early in your career such as "Don't smile until Christmas" and "You have to show them who's boss". We hope you have realised what useless advice this really is.'   (Peter Hook and Andy Vass 2000:20)

6.2 Rogers' three attributes of the effective facilitator

Group leadership has been studied from a number of different perspectives (e.g. within political, psychotherapeutic or work contexts) but the concept that has been most influential in contemporary education is the humanistic notion of the group leader as the 'facilitator'. The concept originates in group psychotherapy, and highlights the importance of the learner in the learning process, while restricting the teacher's role to providing an appropriate climate and resources to support learning. Thus, the teacher is not so much a 'drill sergeant' or 'lecturer of knowledge' as a partner in the learning process.

What is the good facilitator like? In response to this question, humanistic psychologist Carl Rogers (1961) has put forward an influential set of required attributes that has come to be seen as one of the cornerstones of student-centred education. The taxonomy manages to cut through the complexity of the issue by offering a parsimonious and yet comprehensive list of leader characteristics. According to Rogers, in order to function well, facilitators need to possess only three basic attributes: *empathy, acceptance* and *congruence.*

- *Empathy* involves the ability to attend to, interpret and respond to another person's expressions of emotion. In other words, it is the ability to 'get into another person's skin' and to gain a sense of what it is like to be the other person. With regard to the teacher–student relationship, it involves the teacher's getting on the same wavelength as the students and being sensitive to the group atmosphere, motivated by an interest in the welfare of the students.
- *Acceptance*, or as it is often called in psychology, 'unconditional positive regard', involves a non-judgemental, positive attitude towards the students as complex human beings with both virtues and shortcomings (cf. also section 1.3). It is not to be confused with approval: we may accept a person without necessarily approving of everything he or she does. It is a bit like 'loving the sinner, not the sin'.
- Being *congruent* refers to the ability to live, to be and to communicate according to one's true self. It is neither a technique nor an attitude but rather a state of 'realness' and 'authenticity'. The congruent teacher responds as a genuine human being and not as an embodiment of authority statuses and ready-made roles. Being congruent involves being honest with oneself and appropriately honest with one's students even to the extent of admitting at times ignorance, doubt and confusion. If teachers lead students to believe that they know it all, it is hard to remain congruent when we get into unknown territory. Pretending a know-it-all position, even if only to oneself, also adds much undue stress to teaching (see the issue of 'mistakes' further on).

Another take on congruence

'Personal congruence is your ability to have your verbal and non-verbal language fully supported by your beliefs and values. To achieve congruence you will need to be committed to what you are saying and doing.'   (Peter Hook and Andy Vass 2000:46)

We believe that most teachers would, in theory, agree with the benefits of the first two attributes – empathy and acceptance – but the third one, 'congruence', may pose a problem for at least two reasons:

1. Avoiding any pretence also means, as mentioned above, that we need to be open about our limitations. This may seem a controversial issue to many teachers, especially if they do not feel 100 per cent confident in themselves. Uncertainties about one's own knowledge are particularly common amongst non-native teachers of a language who, on the whole, are aware of their linguistic deficiencies and of the all-pervasive nature of their language handicap (Medgyes 2001a). Furthermore, in certain cultures it is simply not done for teachers to admit to mistakes or gaps in their knowledge.
2. Are we supposed to be completely sincere in situations when we are, for example, mad or very disappointed with certain students? Can we really show that we are tired or depressed or have a hangover? Does the teacher have the right to bring in his or her own personal feelings in the teaching process?

These are all valid concerns but there are reasons for thinking otherwise. First, students can usually see through pretension. Both pretending (on the teacher's part) or having to accept pretence (on the students' part) can generate a great deal of tension and can undermine student trust in the leader. Second, although some self-control is important in any situation, this does not mean that we must completely hide our annoyance or disappointment or occasional lack of vitality. In fact, we believe that it is often beneficial to be honest about our feelings: for example, a teacher's open expression of anger or disappointment with some piece of student behaviour may prove to be more effective in getting through to the student than applying some correct disciplinary procedure and thereby reverting to authoritarian distance. Even showing tiredness may create a more authentic atmosphere, potentially eliciting greater student involvement by trying to help to make things work. Having said this, we are also aware of the fact that some cultures have very definite expectations with regard to the infallibility of teachers, which makes it difficult if not impossible to exercise full congruence in them. Yet we trust that even such contexts offer some leeway for adopting at least some of the facilitator's characteristics.

From the journals of a teacher and a student in Taiwan

[Teacher:]

'I used to hide my negative emotions a lot from my classes. More recently I have found that it is better to be up front with my students when I am unhappy about something or even about their behaviour as students. I went in the other day and self-disclosed about my feelings to one class and what a student wrote back was

---

amazing. It contained a lot of the rationale for teachers being human in class [see below] ... The student I do feel may be overgeneralising about foreigners too much, but she's got her hand on the pulse of teacher–student rapport, and good learning environments, and students being partners with teachers.'

[Student:]
'I found that much foreign teachers have a healthier way in expressing their emotions. When most Chinese teachers feel tired or have problems in their personal lives, they often conceal their bad mood and don't let their students know, so if one day the bad becomes too much to hold back, the volcano erupts, and the students feel confused and angry about the teacher's reaction. Because the teacher didn't show any signs of unhappiness so the students don't know that they should take 'preventions' beforehand (such as being more cooperative than usual during the class or not making the teacher angry). I remember that [another foreign teacher] sometimes began a class with an apology, which explained what things happen to him and why he felt unhappy (about us or about other subjects). The same thing that you did. I think it's a very good thing to do, because ... that's the only way we can know how to be our teacher's best partner during the class.'

6.3 Heron's system of facilitation

Although we find Rogers' set of three attributes very important for becoming a group-conscious teacher, the set leaves several issues open about how to behave as a teacher-facilitator. It does not provide, for example, straightforward guidelines about the characteristics of a facilitator with regard to Lewin's distinction of democratic, authoritative and laissez-faire leadership styles. We can perhaps intuitively feel that the 'democratic' style may be the closest to facilitative teaching, but – as argued at the beginning of this chapter – without taking the developmental level of the group into consideration it is difficult to come up with specific principles. Surely, at the beginning of a group's life a teacher cannot be as 'democratic' and 'facilitative' as with a fully matured, cohesive group. This is where it is useful to bring in a fairly simple and straightforward system of operation and control set up by Heron (1999) concerning the behaviour of facilitators.

In *The Complete Facilitator's Handbook*, Heron (1999) argues that – contrary to beliefs – a good facilitator is *not* characterised by a 'soft touch' or a 'free for all' mentality. He distinguishes three different *modes* of facilitation:

- *Hierarchical mode*, whereby the facilitator exercises the power to direct the learning process *for* the group, thinking and acting *on behalf of* the group, and making all the major decisions. In this mode, therefore, the facilitator takes full responsibility for designing the syllabus and providing structures for learning.
- *Cooperative mode*, whereby the facilitator shares the power and responsibilities *with* the group, prompting members to be more self-directing in the various forms of learning. In this mode the facilitator collaborates with the members in devising the learning process, and outcomes are negotiated.
- *Autonomous mode*, whereby the facilitator respects the autonomy of the group in finding their *own* way and exercising their *own* judgement. The task of the facilitator in this mode is to create the conditions within which students' self-determination can flourish.

Heron on the relative value of the three modes of facilitation

Heron (1999) makes it clear that he does not consider any of the three modes of facilitation superior to the others. As he summarises, if there is too much hierarchical control, 'participants become passive and dependent or hostile and resistant. They wane in self-direction, which is the core of all learning. Too much co-operative guidance may degenerate into a subtle kind of nurturing oppression, and may deny the group the benefits of totally autonomous learning. Too much autonomy for participants and laissez-faire on your [i.e. the facilitator's] part, and they may wallow in ignorance, misconception and chaos' (p. 9).

The art of effective facilitation, according to Heron (1999), lies in finding the right balancing and sequencing of the three modes 'as and when appropriate' (p. 8). Accordingly, one attribute of the effective facilitator is the flexibility to move from mode to mode. He gives some guidelines as to how to achieve the right balance. First of all, the three modes do not exclude each other but can be combined even in the same lesson. That is, even in a lesson which is, say, characterised by an autonomous facilitative mode, a certain task may involve increased teacher participation. Or within a hierarchically given exercise, members can be autonomous when taking their turn.

Second, Heron has found that the ideal proportion of the three modes changes with the *level of development* of the group. He distinguishes three stages:

- At the outset of group development, the optimal mode is predominantly *hierarchical*, offering a clear and straightforward framework within which early development of cooperation and autonomy can safely occur. Participants at this stage may be lacking the necessary knowledge and skills to orientate themselves and rely on the leader for guidance. Within the hierarchical mode there should be, however, cooperative exchanges with the teacher and autonomous practice on their own. Also, even in this mode the students' consent should be sought for the major leader-owned decisions.
- Later, in the 'middle phase', more *cooperation* with group members may be appropriate in managing the learning process. The facilitator can negotiate the curriculum with the students and cooperatively guide their learning activities. Their acquired confidence will allow them to take an increasing part in making the decisions about how their learning should proceed.
- Finally, when the group has reached maturity and is thus ready for the *autonomous mode*, more power needs to be delegated to the group in order for members to achieve full self-direction in their learning. Learning contracts (see section 2.5), self-evaluation and peer assessment may 'institutionalise' their independence.

6.4 Hersey and Blanchard's situational-leadership theory

Heron's (1999) system of facilitation bears a close resemblance with one of the best-known theories of leadership in organisational psychology, proposed by Hersey and Blanchard (1982). This theory is based on the distinction of two types of leader behaviour:

- *Relationship behaviour*, which concerns meeting the group members' *personal needs*, and involves behaviours geared at increasing group cohesiveness, reducing interpersonal conflict and boosting the group's morale.
- *Task leadership*, which concerns the *task* the group is facing rather than member satisfaction. It involves behaviours aiming at co-ordinating actions, proposing solutions, setting subtasks, removing barriers, disseminating information and allocating resources.

According to Hersey and Blanchard (1982), during the initial, formation stage of group life members work best with a *high-task/low-relationship* leader. After the group has achieved more maturity and can work smoothly, the leader should increase relationship-oriented behaviour for a *high-task/high-relationship* orientation. As the group further matures, the leader can decrease both types of orientation: task-orientation first, since with moderately mature groups a *high-relation-ship/low-task* style works best. Finally with a fully mature group, a *low-relationship/low-task* orientation is appropriate. Thus, an effective leader needs to demonstrate four different leadership styles during the group's developmental process: *telling, selling, participating* and *delegating.*

1. *Telling* entails providing a task orientation with a clear explanation at the beginning of group life.
2. *Selling* entails convincing students that the tasks are helpful for their learning. However, as the best salespeople know, convincing is a relationship business and improving relationships among the class members is probably one of the best ways to increase the value of the activities in the classroom.
3. *Participating* means allowing students to interact with the material and each other rather than merely listening to the teacher, giving them lots of time on task.
4. *Delegating* entails letting students in on the process of choosing and directing activities. This is when teachers get to learn a lot from their students.

In Vygotskian terms . . .

At first, in the phases referred to by Hersey and Blanchard (1982) as 'telling' and 'selling', students are 'other-regulated' by the teacher in a Vygotskian (1978) perspective. In participating they begin to be 'object regulated' or 'task regulated' by the activity. Once more of the activity selection and structure has been dele-gated, students develop 'self-regulation'. These different ways of conceptualising their increasing participation and takeover of their learning correspond to their developing 'zones of proximal devel-opment' (Vygotsky 1962). They start out with firm leading and modelling on the part of the teacher and shift as students internalise more and more of the processes and teachers learn how to let go.

6.5 A synthesis of the different approaches

The approaches described above come from very different sources: Lewin and his colleagues' distinction of three leadership styles from social psychology; Rogers and Heron's notions of the facilitator from humanistic psychology; and Hersey and Blanchard's situational model from organisational (i.e. work) psychology. Yet, the different perspectives complement each other and we can draw the following general principles from them:

- At the beginning of a group's life students work best if they have detailed guidance from the teacher. This 'controlling' approach resembles to some extent Lewin and his colleagues' 'autocratic' leadership style.
- The controlling approach produces short-term results: productivity and a well-ordered classroom. However, it is not desirable in the long run as it blocks group development and keeps the relationships in the group cool.
- With the maturation of the group, the group-conscious teacher should loosen the grip and rely more on the group's resources. This process is safeguarded by the teacher's increasing rapport with and trust in the students that emerge as a function of the empathy, acceptance and congruence displayed. The result is a more 'democratic' teaching style that involves delegating as many task-management roles to the learners as possible.
- When the group matures and is ready to acquire more interpersonal and group skills, the teacher should further decrease his or her active presence in the group, reaching what might seem a 'laissez-faire' leadership style – but of course, this is a well-prepared withdrawal of the scaffolding rather than an abandonment of leadership responsibilities.
- In sum: a group-conscious teaching style involves an increasing encouragement of and reliance on the group's own resources and the active facilitation of autonomous learning that is in accordance with the maturity level of the group.

Lao-tse on the 'good leader'

'A leader is best when people barely know he exists, not so good when people obey and acclaim him, worst when they despise him. . . . But of a good leader, who talks little when his work is done, his aim fulfilled, they will all say: "We did this ourselves".'

A word of caution: the participatory kind of education we are advocating may be very unusual for some, or many, students; they may not have the motivation or the necessary interpersonal and study skills to take advantage of the opportunities offered to them. As a result, as Heron (1999) warns, students may be neither satisfied nor encouraged when stepping beyond the 'hierarchical' mode. The resolution, he suggests, lies in patience and timing:

> Only give away an appropriate amount of power at a time, otherwise neither you nor the students will be able to cope. And realise the huge array of options you have in combining the three modes in different ways, with varying degrees of emphasis, in relation to so many diverse facets of the educational process. There is no need to hasten inappropriately forward by gross leaps, when you can proceed slowly by innumerable subtle steps.
>
> (p. 11)

6.6 'Transactional' versus 'transformational' leadership

The discussion of basic leadership issues would not be complete without describing a recently made important distinction between 'transactional' and 'transformational' leadership. According to Bass and Avolio (1994), most leaders are transactional rather then transformational. This means that they treat their relationship with their group as a transaction: they set goals and offer rewards for achievement or punishment for unsatisfactory performance. While transactional leaders can be very effective in a wide variety of settings, particularly when things are going generally well and no major changes are needed, transformational leadership goes beyond this 'routine' setup and considerably augments transactional leadership. Transformational leaders provide vision and inspiration to the members so that they can transcend their ordinary achievement level and 'go the extra mile' in the service of the collective interest (Brown 2000). The following list of the four main features of transformational leaders explains why we believe that, ideally, good language teachers ought to display as many transformational characteristics as possible:

- *Idealised influence:* Transformational leaders have convictions and represent high standards of ethical and moral conduct. They take stands on difficult issues and emphasise the importance of purpose, commitment and ethics in reaching their decisions. They urge members to adopt their values and strive for the projected vision even at the expense of their self-interests; in 'return', they consider the needs of others over their own personal needs and often set an example by their own sacrifices. As a consequence, such leaders are trusted and respected, and group members identify with them and want to emulate them. Thus, this component refers to a general *charismatic* role modelling function.

- *Inspirational motivation:* Transformational leaders behave in ways that motivate those around them. They express an appealing vision of the future, representing high standards, and communicate this vision clearly in order to build an emotional commitment in their followers; they get the group members involved in envisioning attractive future states. They are also inspirational in their modelling optimism and enthusiasm, and in providing encouragement.
- *Intellectual stimulation:* Transformational leaders question old assumptions and traditions and provide new angles. They stimulate their followers' efforts to be creative and innovative, and encourage them to develop new ideas and view their work from new perspectives. Mistakes are not criticised but are seen as positive signs of taking risks in stepping further.
- *Individualised consideration:* Transformational leaders are sensitive to the members' individual needs, abilities and aspirations. They listen attentively and are concerned with the person's development. They act as coach or mentor.

Thus, transformational leadership, in contrast to transactional leadership, aims at more than the compliance or agreement of the group members; it involves empowering them and producing shifts in their beliefs and values. Transformational leaders care for the participants and motivate them to perform beyond standard expectations of performance. The important aspect of transformational leaders from the perspective of this book is that they achieve their influence by building consensus and pulling the *whole group* along rather than focusing on a few individual disciples/apprentices. That is, they are able to increase the participants' commitment towards a *collective* mission and vision, while also promoting group cohesiveness (cf. Jung and Sosik 2002).

While we find the transformational leadership style appealing in general, we agree with Jordan (2001) that maximum effectiveness can be achieved by combining aspects of transformational and transactional leadership. The way we see it, transformational leaders – such as preachers or presidents – choose distinct moments to attempt transformation. Similarly, it is more ecological for teachers to choose certain moments to enact personal transformation (e.g. at storytelling time) and, at the same time, they also need to set up transactional structures that have the long-term potential of transformation without much of the teacher's direct input (e.g. action logs and newsletters – see sections 7.6 and 8.1).

What are the prerequisites to adopting characteristics of the transformational leader? In the following we would like to emphasise four attributes: *trust in the group, enthusiasm, commitment to the students' learning* and skills in *building rapport with the students.*

Trust in the group

A basic requirement for taking learners beyond the expected level of achievement is the belief that they *can* do it if they try – in other words, the teacher's *trust* in the group. Students have to gain confidence in their ability to actualise their own capacity and, consequently, in the reality of the goal. This confidence-building process is fuelled by the teacher-leader's trust in them (Rogers 1970). At the same time, as discussed earlier, trust is also a key issue in effective group facilitation in the sense that at certain points a teacher must let the group have a real voice in class decisions. 'Going through the motions of group participation and group decision-making but subtly retaining all control is simply manipulation' (Luft 1984:183).

Is it realistic to have such a trust in the group? Yes. A basic assumption in group dynamics is the belief that every group has the potential to structure itself organically and develop into a cohesive unit unless certain external influences block or distort the developmental process. The leader's task, therefore, is not so much to lead the group as to facilitate its evolution by creating the right conditions for development – in particular a safe and accepting climate – and to enable the group to do away with the emerging obstacles (Rogers 1970). That is, the group can do it if allowed.

Enthusiasm

In a thought-provoking article, American psychologist Mihaly Csikszentmihalyi (1997) argues that the teachers who really make a difference in the students' life are the *enthusiastic ones*, the ones who love their subject matter and who show by their dedication and their passion that there is nothing else on earth they would rather be doing. Students might make fun of this dedication but deep inside, Csikszent-mihalyi maintains, they admire that passion. In accordance with this argument, 'enthusiasm' has for long been mentioned as one of the most important ingredients of effective teaching. Enthusiastic teachers convey a great sense of commitment to and excitement about the subject matter content, not only in words but by body language; they 'radiate a "winning" attitude' (McCormick 1994:8). This attitude is 'infectious' – that is, it instils in students a similar willingness to pursue knowledge and make the group successful.

Jere Brophy (1998) adds a further important ingredient to the enthusiasm issue. He emphasises that in our communication with the students we should take it for granted that the students *share* our enthusiasm for learning. We should make explicit references to this. In this way, as Brophy argues, 'To the extent that you *treat students as if they already are eager learners*, they will be more likely to become eager learners. Let them know that they are expected to be curious . . .' (p. 170).

Commitment to student learning

A basic lesson from psychotherapeutic groups is that the more important the members consider the group, the more effective it becomes (Yalom 1995). We have found this to be true not only of the student-members but also of the teacher-leader. It might sound an exaggeration, yet we believe that the extent of the group's commitment to its goals reflects closely that of the teacher. If the teacher is committed to the group goals, so will the group be. After all, in their position of group leader, teachers embody the class spirit. Therefore, a third prerequisite to becoming a 'transformational leader' is that the teacher should be fully committed to making the learning process successful.

Let us add something here. Students may need time to be convinced that you are really on their side. As Hook and Vass (2000) warn us below, we need to actively build up the students' trust over time:

> Do not assume that students will automatically trust that what you are doing is in their best interest. Their previous experiences of adults, both in and out of education, may lead them to very different conclusions. Be consistent. Be predictable. Make sure that you always demonstrate that you have the best interests of your students at heart. Show an interest in them as people both in and out of your classroom. Accept that both you and they have 'off days'. Trust is something that develops over time.　　　　　　　　　　　　　　　　　　　　　(p. 63)

If students sense that the teacher doesn't care . . .

'One of the surest ways of undermining the cohesive structure of groups is for the leader to be absent from the group, either physically or with respect to ongoing interest. Once the group agrees that the leader is not fully supportive of the goals of the group or of its implementation of activities, it . . . becomes fragmented.'　　　　　　　　　　　　　　　　(Henry Kellerman 1981:16)

Building rapport with the students

We don't think that for the readers of this book it requires much justification that it is important for a teacher to have a positive relationship with the students on a personal and not just on an academic level. Teachers who share warm, personal interactions with their students, who respond to their concerns in an empathic manner and who succeed to establish relationships of mutual trust and respect with the learners, are more likely to inspire them in academic matters than those who have no personal ties with the learners. In addition to this, from the perspective of group dynamics, rapport with the students is also important because if it is there, the process of your leadership – that is, the nature of influence that you possess – is significantly enhanced.

Well said . . .

'By establishing rapport, you are making an essential connection with someone at an emotional level. You are willing to share part of you and they are prepared to invest themselves into the dynamic.'   (Peter Hook and Andy Vass 2000:20)

So how do we build rapport? The key element is that students should feel that you are genuinely interested in them; that you pay personal attention to them. Of course, everybody will understand that with a whole class to look after, you cannot spend too much time with individual students, but Dörnyei (2001b) lists a variety of small gestures that do not take up much time yet which can convey personal attention:

- Greet students and remember their names.
- Smile at them.
- Notice interesting features of their appearance (e.g. new haircut).
- Learn something unique about each student and occasionally mention it to them.
- Ask them about their lives outside school.
- Show interest in their hobbies.
- Express in your comments that you've thought about them and that their individual effort is recognised.
- Refer back to what you have talked about before.
- Recognise birthdays.
- Move around in class.
- Include personal topics and examples about students in discussing content matters.
- Send notes/homework to absent students.

6.7 Promoting learner autonomy

'Autonomy' is currently a buzzword in educational psychology – it is also discussed under the label of 'self-regulation' – and during the past decade several books and articles have been published on its significance in the L2 field as well (see Benson 2001, for a recent review). Zoltán has explained this popularity as follows (Dörnyei 2001b:103):

> Allowing a touch of cynicism, I would say that part of the popularity of the concept amongst researchers is due to the fact that educational organisations in general have been rather resistant to the kind of changes that scholars would have liked to see implemented, and research has therefore increasingly turned to analysing how to prepare learners to succeed *in spite of* the education they receive.

Regardless of whether this is a contributing reason, the significance attached to autonomy and self-regulation in recent learning theories coincides with the significance attached to autonomy from a group perspective. The general conclusion emerging from the previous sections is that a group-conscious teaching style involves an increasing reliance on the group's own resources and the active facilitation of autonomous learning. The group's internal development and growing maturity go hand in hand with the members' taking on increasing responsibility and control over their own functioning. In other words, one of the central issues in a group-sensitive teaching practice is the delegation of power and the gradual promotion of learner autonomy. According to Dörnyei (2001b), this may involve using the following strategies, incrementally at first and then more in the performing stage:

- Allow learners *choices* about as many aspects of the learning process as possible, for example about activities, teaching materials, topics, assignments, due dates, the format and the pace of their learning, the arrangement of the furniture, or the peers they want to work with. Choice is the essence of responsibility as it permits learners to see that they are in charge of the learning experience.
- Give students positions of *genuine authority*. Designating course responsibilities makes students fully functioning members of the class group. In traditional school settings such responsibilities are not clearly separated because the teacher takes care of all of them. However, there is no reason why many of the teacher's administrative and management functions could not be turned into student or committee responsibilities. The various leadership roles, committee memberships and other privileges can then be rotated to give everyone a chance.

- Encourage *student contributions and peer teaching*. In our experience learners are very resourceful about finding ways to convey new material to their peers. They also learn more when they teach each other – this is what Palincsar and Brown (1984) refer to as 'reciprocal teaching'.
- Encourage *project work*. When students are given complete projects to carry out, they will function in an autonomous way by definition: the teacher is not part of the immediate communication network and students are required to organise themselves, to decide on the most appropriate course of action to achieve the goal and to devise the way in which they report their findings back to the class.
- When appropriate, allow learners to use *self-assessment* procedures (cf. Ekbatani and Pierson 2000; Murphey 1994). Self-assessment raises the learners' awareness about the mistakes and successes of their own learning, and gives them a concrete sense of participation in the learning process. Of course, in most school contexts self-assessment may not be considered legitimate by the management – in such cases students may perhaps be involved in at least deciding *when* and *how* to be evaluated.

Just imagine . . .

'Imagine the sheer joy of teaching a course in which the students work up a reading list, pre-circulate the materials, make brief presentations to the group, lead the group sessions, and grade one another's papers. What would we do? We would assist students to find appropriate literature and coach them in making presentations and in leading the small group. We would make comments on the process and ensure that the goals were being met.'

(Richard Tiberius 1999:166)

It is important to reiterate that most students will not be ready to participate in the above strategic processes aiming for increasing autonomy without any prior preparation. These strategies will be more successful when they are implemented incrementally and students are provided with scaffolded steps to experience their success in them (Murphey and Jacobs 2000). For example, before students actually give themselves a grade on a test, we might ask them to evaluate activities done in class and the amount they learned from them, thereby 'training' their metacognitive and self-regulatory skills.

6.8 Summary

In this chapter we have covered the following main points:

- Leadership matters; by becoming more aware of what effective leadership entails, we can lead our class groups more effectively.
- One leadership style is not necessarily better than another; it depends on what stage the group is at and what the group needs at certain moments in time.
- Generally, it is recommended that group-conscious teaching begins more autocratically to give direction, security and impetus to the group. Then as the students begin performing, teachers can initiate increasing democratic control of the processes. When the group further matures and begins to show their initiative, more autonomy-inviting leadership might be the most conducive to encouraging student independence and initiative.
- Certain circumstances during the life of a group may warrant the leadership style of another stage; for example, even with a mature group, when introducing a totally new activity, the teacher might be autocratic at first in order to model it appropriately and show students that it works.
- Empathy, acceptance and congruence are the three attributes of the effective facilitator.
- Rather than simply doing a job as a transactional leader, a *transformational* leader educates for life and motivates the group to perform beyond standard expectations of performance.
- There are (at least) four prerequisites to becoming more *transformational* in our leadership role: trust in the group, enthusiasm about the subject matter, commitment to the students' learning and skills in building rapport with them.
- One of the goals of an effective leader is to lead so well as to no longer be needed at times, generating student and group collaborative autonomy. This autonomy needs scaffolding and can be done in many ways. However, the leader is still a valuable contributing member of the group and should not abdicate completely but rather balance the handing over of more and more responsibility to the learners with his or her own valuable input.

> *Important questions about group leadership*
> - Who were the teachers that you respected most and what kind of leaders were they?
> - In retrospect, when did your teachers, coaches or other leaders

shift styles of leadership? How and why did that happen? What were the results?
- What kind of leader are you generally? Which leadership style suits you best? What can you do to improve in the style that least suits you?
- How can teachers show trust, commitment and enthusiasm to a class? How might you have done this already?
- How can teachers 'let go' and hand over more control to the students? How difficult would you find this personally?

7 Student roles and role modelling

This chapter will:

- *describe what student roles are and how they affect group life;*
- *present techniques for teachers to increase the effectiveness and productivity of their classes by inviting or assigning specific student roles;*
- *introduce the concept of 'role modelling' and how it can be used to promote learning.*

> **Think about it first**
>
> What kind of roles have you noticed your students taking in your classes? What kind of roles have you invited students to take in your classes? Think of a few students in your classes that would be good role models for the other students.

'Role' as a technical term originally comes from sociology and refers to the shared expectation of how an individual should behave. In other words, roles describe what people are supposed to do. This meaning, in fact, is very close to the more common usage of the word that refers to an actor's role in theatre performances: enacting a certain role there means behaving in a way that meets the expectations of the director and the audience with regard to the particular character. The term has also been widely used in group dynamics – hence this chapter in this book – because scholars have long recognised that every member fills at least one role in a group and that this role greatly determines how the person will function. There is a general agreement that roles are of great importance with regard to the life and productivity of the group: if students are cast in a good role, they will become useful members of the team, they will perform necessary and complementary functions and, at the same time, they will be satisfied with their self-image and contribution. However, an inappropriate role can lead to personal conflict and will work against the cohesiveness and effectiveness of the group.

About a good group – from an interview with a student

Everybody knew what their task was, what role they had in the group, and that they could contribute to the group's success with their own task. Thus, everybody behaved naturally; we could be ourselves; and this made the group a good one.

(Ehrman & Dörnyei 1998:146)

Roles can be divided into two main types: 'naturally emerging roles' (or *informal* roles) and 'assigned roles' (or *formal* roles). An example for the first is the *class clown*, and for the second the *group secretary* appointed by the teacher. In this chapter we will first look at the first type, the 'unofficial' roles, and then we will examine the capacity for teachers to encourage group functioning through inviting or assigning student roles in the classroom. The overall message of this chapter is that roles are basic building blocks for successful class performance: a highly performing class group will display a balanced set of complementary and constructive student roles, and teachers, by their own communications and the structures of their activities, can encourage students to explore and assume different roles and adopt the ones that suit them best.

What about your roles?

You yourself may sometimes become aware of filling certain roles in certain groups. At committee meetings, Tim for example typically notices that he often becomes the distracter or clown as he tosses juggling balls to different teachers and notices alternative potential meanings of what the speaker is saying. However, as a teacher he finds himself turning into more of a leader, trying to calm distracters like himself. Similarly, at the beginning of his university teaching career, Zoltán often played the role of the rebel at his department until one day he was assigned a position of leadership and found others rebelling against him (so he quickly resigned . . .). What about you? Think of the various groups that you belong to (e.g. professional, sports, recreational or family groups). How would you define your roles? Which is the most comfortable and the most uncomfortable one to enact?

7.1 Informal roles

At the beginning of group life everybody starts with a clear slate and is equal with regard to the group's role system – this of course only applies to the students and not the teacher, who is the official group leader. However, very soon a process of role differentiation begins and a variety of group roles develop: there emerge, for example, those who seem to lead, those who clown, and those who simply wish to follow. These informal roles evolve out of the trial-and-error process: the members of the group 'teach' individuals which behaviours are appropriate and which are not by rewarding and punishing the trials (Wilson 2002). Although the emerging roles are not unchangeable, and anybody may shift between various roles at different times, a person often takes on one particular role unconsciously and sticks to it most of the time in a particular group. In fact, it has been found that roles, once established, tend to persist. They can become such powerful components of the classroom tapestry that, as Forsyth (1999) points out, if the person who has held a certain role departs, the role itself often remains and will be filled by another member.

Although listing all the possible roles is impossible, some typical examples include the leader, the organiser, the energiser, the harmoniser, the complainer, the scapegoat, the pessimist, the rebel, the clown and the outcast (for more details, see below). Some roles are found in nearly every group, such as the leader or the newcomer. For example, a 'newcomer' is expected to be anxious, passive, dependent and conforming, and the more effectively new group members play this role, the faster they will be accepted by old-timers (Levine and Moreland 1990). Other roles are specific to a particular group's unique composition or task.

Tim's account of his juggling classes

I often give one-day lessons in 'Juggling as a Metaphor for Learning' in secondary schools. I like to arrive before the students and watch them come into the classroom. As they walk in and sit and socialise before the presentation, I can already see certain members sticking out as being attractive to others and others who are more like 'loners' and 'clowns'. If I have time I might go and talk to the potential leaders myself and ask them about their class and interests. I might also talk to the loners and clowns to let them know I see them and acknowledge their presence. Often while doing so I will toss them a juggling ball and let them know a bit about what we will be doing that day. The ball then is literally in

---

their hands. As I walk away, other students begin asking them about the ball and what we will be doing. With the natural leaders, their role as a leader is confirmed and the class is led to the topic more congruently. But sometimes even the simple fact that I have given a ball to a loner or clown drives them into the role of being a leader as others ask about the ball and they enter into the 'knower' role.

When it comes to the time for a juggling demonstration, I don't take the leader; I take the clown. If I don't take the clown they will be competing with me anyway for the floor. So I give them the floor and bring them up front and quite honestly usually have a wonderful time laughing and joking with them as they learn how to juggle. Sometimes, but not always, the clown is transformed for a while after the successful demonstration and becomes an expert, a kind of leader, which may continue long after the class if they like the role and others accept it.

As students begin to repeat the juggling demonstration in pairs, they each have the opportunity to be leaders and make suggestions in their small groups of two. Working in pairs, for juggling or conversations, allows all students to exercise, awaken and enhance their capabilities to lead (and for overpowering leaders to exercise their ability to follow occasionally). When I see two clowns/distracters together, I often separate them and give them non-clown partners because I know how I myself can get carried away with another clown as a partner.

Student leaders

A key role in every group is the 'leader'. In educational settings we can talk about two types of leadership. The first is the role of *explicit, official leader*, appointed by the authorities, which is almost always the teacher (although in some countries there are also appointed student leaders). Their characteristics and leadership functions were described in the previous chapter. The second type of leadership is that which emerges spontaneously – in most classrooms students take *unofficial leadership roles*. It is these unofficial student leaders that we are going to examine now.

When teachers look carefully in the first few classes, they can often see the unconscious leaders in the room. Other students look at these leaders when questions arise as to what to do and they tend to group around them unconsciously. When the leader sighs and looks bored, the other students tend to do the same. When the leader is excited and interested, other students tend to become passionate as well. If teachers are aware of such leaders early on, they can get into rapport with them and find out what motivates them (gets them excited and interested). Then they can associate their teaching with their motivations and many others in the class may join in more smoothly and invest themselves in the learning process. This approach, however, is not without dangers: while it may ensure the smooth functioning of the group, by siding with the student-leaders the teacher may become instrumental in diverting attention away from quieter students, thereby pushing them further into the background. Thus, as in so many cases, the teacher's sensitivity in dealing with the group is indispensable.

Student leaders emerge in most groups, certainly the well-functioning ones, and their contribution to facilitating the efficient functioning of the group has been recognised as being as important as that of formally designated leadership (De Souza and Klein 1995). Typically, two types of student leaders emerge, corresponding to the two main needs a group has:

- *task specialists*;
- *socio-emotional specialists*.

Task specialists are concerned with trying to move the group towards accomplishing its goals; in doing so, they display organisational skills and do a lot of prodding and nudging of group members to prompt them into action. Often they must engage in unpleasant duties such as giving orders, criticising or stopping members from doing something. While all these actions may be necessary for the group to reach the goal, they create tensions and negative reactions. This is why very often a second type of natural leader emerges, the *socio-emotional specialist*, who can be seen as the peacekeeper because their main task is to maintain harmony within the group. Thus, the emergence of task and socioemotional leaders is a natural consequence of the two basic, and partly conflicting demands within the group: to get on with the job and to maintain cohesiveness. Ehrman and Dörnyei (1998:177) quote an extract from an interview with a student about a young adult learner group she has been part of, which very clearly illustrates this duality:

> *It was very good at the beginning that there were ready roles, that is, there was a girl who was very warm-hearted and liked giving presents, so she became a kind of tacit mother-of-the-group, and the young man was the one who had the responsibility for organising us.*

It is obvious from the above discussion that we see the emergence of student leaders as a very positive sign from the group's point of view. Although inexperienced or authoritative teachers may see them as challenges to their authority, the sharing of leadership functions between the official and unofficial leaders is both natural and necessary. Groups can benefit a great deal if you can treat the student leaders as partners who work towards the same goal as you. Of course, negative student leadership can also occur; techniques to deal with disruptive or deviant students or cliques are discussed in Chapters 2 and 8.

Other common classroom roles

In the previous section we mentioned the two main needs of the group: to accomplish tasks and to maintain good relationships. Besides the student leaders who take overall charge of these functions, we can see a whole variety of more specialised group roles that emerge for catering for these two needs. Accordingly, informal group roles have tradition-ally been divided in the literature into *task roles* and *social roles*, the latter referring to group building and group maintenance. This division has stood the test of time because there is a natural tendency for people to gravitate toward one or the other, with few people being able to specialise in both. The most common naturally emerging *task roles* are:

- *Initiator/contributor*, who pushes the group to get on with the task and offers new ways to approach the problem.
- *Information seeker/provider*, who seeks and provides outside in-formation and resources to serve as background knowledge for the group members.
- *Opinion seeker/giver*, who elicits the members' feelings and reactions and also provides their own.
- *Elaborator/clarifier*, who takes others' ideas/points and embroiders upon them (e.g. rephrases or illustrates them, or looks at some further implications) to make them more useful to the group.
- *Coordinator*, who makes sure that things stay on schedule and ideas remain relevant to the initial problem/task.
- *Evaluator/critic*, who appraises the various suggestions in order to make sure that the best ideas are used in the task.
- *Energiser*, who does not allow the attention or group energy level to flag, by providing encouragement and personal example.
- *Secretary/recorder*, who takes notes to prevent ideas from being forgotten or lost.

Group maintenance roles whose function is to satisfy the group's socioemotional dimension include:

- *Encourager/supporter*, who offers praise and agreement, and who provides backing for the ideas of shy members.
- *Harmoniser*, who helps to resolve tensions by telling jokes and mediating conflicts.
- *Compromiser*, who helps to shift the various positions to create unity.
- *Feeling expresser*, who airs emotions that are lurking in the background.
- *Equaliser*, who makes sure that everyone is included to an equal extent by setting up procedures, drawing out some individuals and limiting domination by others.

Besides the above roles that are directly related to the group's needs, there are some others which either do not fit neatly into this dual system, or which are related to individual needs, often at the group's expense. Examples of the first type are the *follower*, which is a low-profile constructive role, as well as the *clown* and the *scapegoat*, which will be elaborated on below. Disruptive individual roles include the *blocker/nitpicker*, who never agrees to anything; the *aggressor*, who picks fights; the *dominator*, who is interested in exerting his own influence; the *recognition seeker*, the *bragger* and the *self-confessor*, who constantly seek attention. These roles all have in common that they concern jockeying status, attention or power for the individual who plays them. Instead of contributing to the group's goals, they prevent the group from achieving goals by taking up group time and energy, and by being distracting and/or disruptive.

Harnessing the headstrong . . .

'From time to time most language teachers come across "difficult" students who demand attention in a variety of ways, including asking strings of questions, sabotaging group activities by refusing to cooperate, or charismatically leading splinter groups astray at the back of the class . . . It appears that experienced teachers with intuition are often able to find roles for strong-willed students, thereby harnessing their valuable energy for positive, group-building ends . . . Having a recognised role appeared to give them a sense of responsibility towards their classes, so that their behaviour was group-enhancing rather than group-destroying. These roles could include helping weaker students; being the class grammar expert; being the quickest person at checking word meanings in the dictionary; telling the teacher the time of TV programmes for the class to watch; being the person who could be relied upon to make a quick joke; being the class organiser for outside activities.'

(Rose Senior 1997:8)

Clowns

The *clown* is such a typical role in school settings that it warrants a more detailed description. There is hardly a class which does not have its resident clown. Some people love to clown, and shift into this powerful role even if they decide not to. However, clowning is not just an individual inclination; the group also needs clowns. They bring in humour, which helps the group relax and attend to the task. In this sense, the clown plays a positive role, that of the 'harmoniser' described above. The problem with clowning is that it very easily gets out of hand – clowns often find it difficult to stop and the group can easily get caught up in clowning even if they regret it later. When this happens and the role turns into horseplay or ham acting, it becomes self-serving and can seriously distract from the productivity.

Scapegoats

One of Zoltán's postgraduate students used to make ends meet by professional sailing. His accounts about how he and his crew took around millionaires for long holiday cruises in the Mediterranean or Caribbean were fascinating, but there was one thing in these accounts that was particularly noteworthy: he explained that *every* crew he had been part of, whether as the captain or as an ordinary crew member, had a *scapegoat*. Someone everybody blamed for any mistakes made. And there was always only *one* scapegoat at a time; the others seemed to get along with each other just fine.

Zoltán's student did not know anything about the theory of group dynamics, yet his account is consistent with psychological analyses of scapegoating. As Ehrman and Dörnyei (1998) describe, the scapegoat is amongst the most conflictual of roles at the group level. In most cases scapegoats are actually not responsible for all they are being blamed for – rather, they are used by the group to diffuse some other tensions. For example, scapegoating can involve displacing aggression from another person like the leader onto someone else whose displeasure is much less dangerous. We suspect that with sailing this was indeed the case: the crew took out on the scapegoat the tension that had been generated by the stark contrast between their extremely hard work and the oblivious luxury of their over-privileged passengers.

Other times, groups either permit or induce a likely member to become a spokesperson for the feelings and thoughts that most of the group members would like to disavow but, at the same time, because others' needs are not being met, that individual also becomes a focus for resentment. It is so convenient to settle issues by claiming, 'If only that person were not here, things would go very well.' Scapegoats, then, may be socially rejected, ridiculed, abused or even thrown out of the group. Remarkably, as Ehrman and Dörnyei argue (1998), if a scapegoat is expelled from the group, a new scapegoat is often 'recruited', usually someone else who represents another unwanted feeling for the group.

7.2 Inviting and assigning student roles

In this part we want to suggest that rather than simply letting roles emerge in a class, we might encourage role taking through using certain teaching structures, strategies and activities. There are two degrees of this more conscious effort: we can either *encourage* role taking or we can actually *assign* students certain roles.

Encouraging role taking

We believe that in order for anybody to become a 'fully-fledged' member of the group, they need to assume a role that is recognised by all the other group members. This is relatively easy for extroverts, whose powerful presence cannot be ignored for long. However, other shyer students, particularly if their language proficiency is not out-standing, will find it difficult to get into the flow and might be stuck on the periphery of the group. In their cases, it might be necessary to apply some specific encouragement to take on an individual role. There are several opportunities for doing so and initially it does not really matter what these roles are as long as they create a positive social image. In an insightful analysis, Rose Senior (1997), for example, reports on a student who regularly arrived late, which after a while caused the class to burst into spontaneous, whole-group laughter. This rather unusual role was instrumental in heightening the student's self-esteem and integrating him into the group. A similar function was achieved with another student, who never had the right books, which led to gentle teacher teasing and a positive group feeling. Even someone's frequent language mistakes could be turned into a positive group contribution because they provided the opportunity for everyone in the class to learn. Mind you, one must strike a delicate balance here – before the teacher in question capitalised on a certain student's pronunciation errors, she first demonstrated to the class how difficult she found it to pronounce words in the student's mother tongue.

Becoming language

Encouraging role taking involves noticing and reinforcing any tentative role attempts on the students' part, and sometimes even highlighting possible roles that a particular marginal learner may assume. Needless to say, all this needs to be done in a subtle way; we imagine that positive remarks such as the following might just do the trick:

'Great, Yasmin. Thanks for the clarification. You are very good at noticing things.'

'That was another very useful personal illustration, Peter. Thanks – we all appreciate it.'

'Yuki, you really led your group well in that activity. You are a leader!'

'Lee, I like the way you confirm your classmates by summarising what they say. You really make them feel good about contributing.'

'You ask very good questions, Mari. That helps us to consider many important points.'

For more tips on how to encourage role taking, see section 7.5 on 'self-fulfilling prophecies'.

Assigning students specific roles

In her influential book on group work, Elizabeth Cohen (1994) asks the question of how efficient learning groups avoid the notorious problems of non-participation and interpersonal difficulty (e.g. domination by one member). The secret of their success, she concludes, lies to a large extent in the way 'members have something specific to do' (p. 87). She has generally found that members feel very satisfied with their part in the group process in groups with different roles and/or jobs to do, and such groups work efficiently, smoothly and productively. Cohen then argues that 'When each person's job is given a name and is accompanied by a list of expected behaviours, group members have been assigned specific roles to play' (p. 87). In this section we will look at these assigned roles and how role assignment works best.

Of course, 'assigning roles' is not a new concept for many language teachers, because in communicative language teaching activities 'role play' has become a standard task, and this involves giving students specific roles (often on cue cards), such as the greengrocer, the retired businessman or the television reporter. However, the roles Cohen (1994) is talking about are very different from these in that they do not concern the task content but rather *how* the work is to be done, involving important functions such as:

- initiating a task;
- asking for and giving information;
- reformulating, clarifying;
- giving examples;
- confronting (acting as the 'devil's advocate');
- synthesising and summarising;
- time-keeping;
- chairing;
- keeping the discussion to the point;
- ensuring everybody's involvement;
- encouraging and tension-relieving;
- taking notes and recording results.

These functions are similar to the naturally emerging, informal roles that were discussed in section 7.1 above. The difference is that by consciously assigning particular roles to members in small groups or in the general class, we speed up the natural process and make sure that the resulting role pattern best supports the group and suits the task in question. We have also found that role allocation increases the learning potential of the group and fosters the development of abilities in different members. By separating and highlighting specific functions, we allow the scaffolding of small roles at first so that students can learn them and become comfortable with them. Later students may enact the roles naturally without any conscious assigning.

Role assignment has further positive effects. When students are unsure as to their roles, they can feel a lot of stress and they can also spend a lot of time figuring out roles in a group. Thus, giving them roles to start with is beneficial as it provides security and saves (usually awkward) time. Furthermore, when accompanied with the job descriptions and examples of what participants might say, role allocation can contribute effectively to teaching the language that is needed to interact smoothly. The roles may not match the students' natural tendencies to lead or follow quietly, but they do encourage more interpersonal management and adjusting to one another. For example, when asked if they preferred having the roles or not, Carl, a Taiwanese student, responded, 'I preferred to have them because it's fun to play different roles at one class. Also, the role appointed helped us to identify ourselves in the discussion.' Another learner, Brian, highlighted the different language and communicative intent in each role: 'I like the exercise. It lets me know that different roles have different communicative way in discussion.'

What kind of roles are we talking about? In the table below we have listed some of the most useful roles that might be assigned to students during the course of a variety of tasks.

Some useful student roles

- *Facilitator:* Organises the other members; sees to it that everyone gets the help they need; keeps the group on task.
- *Encourager:* Encourages everybody to say something; solicits contributions from each member.
- *Harmoniser:* Smoothes out problems; eases interpersonal conflicts; promotes compromises; does not allow 'put-downs'.
- *Recorder/reporter:* Writes up what the group has found out or produced; acts as an announcer or narrator.
- *Summariser:* Summarises what other people have said on paper; highlights key ideas and disagreements to be resolved.
- *Checker:* Makes sure that everybody in the group understands what is to be learned and that everybody has finished their individual task.
- *Resource person:* Moves around the classroom collecting materials and helps the group use these materials.
- *Information-getter:* Communicates with other groups and the teacher to receive advice, feedback and further information.
- *Time-keeper:* Makes sure that the group makes appropriate progress in the allotted time period.

An interesting account by Pawan and Jacobson (in press) indicates that even in an internet-based, online distance education class, role-assignments might be constructively used to assure more equilateral participation and learning. As the authors describe:

> Similar to classroom discussions, in our asynchronous discussion, we frequently have some students dominating discussions while others are merely reading (lurking) but not participating in discussions. To address this, we establish the following roles for students to assume each week: starters, provocateurs and wrappers. Students take turns assuming these roles. 'Starters' are responsible for raising issues from the weekly readings, asking questions, and encouraging class

members to make connections between what they read and their experiences. Most importantly, the starters are to keep everybody on track in their discussions. 'Provocateurs' are to provide a contrary perspective and to challenge opinions. Finally 'wrappers' are to pull discussion themes together at the end and suggest readings for future reference and discussion.

In order to test how this idea works, in one of his classes Tim followed Pawan and Jacobson's example and provided students with the following role descriptions:

Initiator: Your job is to introduce the topic and explain it for the others briefly. Set the stage. But also encourage the others to talk. Invite them when necessary ('So what do you think about this, John?'). Some other things you might say are: 'Well, I think this statement means that . . .'; 'I think the research on this shows that . . .'; 'My personal opinion about that is that . . .'; 'What do you think?'; 'What are your personal experiences that have to do with this statement?'.

Provocateur: Your job is to state your opinion but to also question things to make people think about the opposites or alternative points of view. Be polite but question things, dig a little deeper. You might say things like, 'What evidence do we have that this is true or false?'; 'Should we just believe what we think, or our past experience, or what the book says?'; 'How do you know that?'; 'Why do you think that?'; 'Do you think that most people would agree with you?'; 'What would people who disagree say for their reasons?'.

Wrapper ('wrap up' means to finish it – time to pack it up and go): Your job is to keep time and to make sure you have at least time to summarise at the end. Each statement can be discussed for ___ minutes. You can still participate in the ongoing discussion but you should also bring everything together at the end. You might say things like: 'Time is almost up for us on this statement so let me summarise'; 'OK, let me see if I understood everything that we said'; 'Let me tell you what I have in my notes'; 'First XXX said that . . . Then YYY said . . . But we didn't quite agree whether . . . or not. Finally, we decided that . . .'. It is OK not to have resolved things by the end. You just report that.

Tim then had students rotate roles periodically with discussion questions. He was actually amazed at how well it worked and how much the students embraced the roles. The role assignments gave them clear tasks to be accomplished and permission to participate in specific ways that enabled the group to speed through the discussion profitably rather than squander valuable classroom time being afraid of voicing their opinions and critically thinking.

Marie shows in her comment below that students can be conscious that filling certain roles may be difficult for them, but at the same time they can learn how to play different roles: '[In the collaborative activity] I can focus on my defects and look at other people's merits. For example, I didn't do well to be a wrapper. I could learn what I should improve from my partners.' Joan also emphasises the learning from her peers in the collaborative activities: 'Both my partners are good initiators and provocateurs. They explain the ideas and express their thoughts pretty clearly. And they are so well-organised. I learned a lot from them.' Thus, the benefits of training learners for different roles are not restricted to smooth group function but also involve giving all participants experience with different roles over time and the opportunity to learn from their classmates' examples and receive feedback on their performance as members of a group.

7.3 Role problems

With all the good things mentioned about roles, you might say, what's the catch? Here is a list:

- *Role ambiguity:* Because various natural roles emerge without a formal 'job description', the responsibilities of the roles are often ill-defined. A person playing a role might have a different understanding of how to behave from what the others expect. This will obviously create uncertainty and stress in the person and some potential frustration on the others' part because the role is not being performed the way they desire.
- *Role conflict:* We often occupy different roles in different groups or even within the same group in different situations. These may involve conflicting demands. A classic example is the problematic nature of the teacher socialising with more mature students, thus becoming the 'boss' and a 'mate' at the same time. But this conflict is not restricted to such extreme cases: task and socio-emotional roles (see section 7.1) might also disagree with each other. Conflict can also be caused by the different status of one's various roles, for instance when an adult executive becomes a language student. (However, executives may be allowed to continue to see themselves as the leader, though, in one-to-one tutoring where others cannot see them and they can somewhat direct the tutor; Murphey 1991.)
- *Role distance:* When an individual experiences a role as inconsistent

with his or her self-image, the individual may signal in one way or another that the role is 'not me'. The executive-turned-language student may talk constantly of past business successes in order to distance him or herself from the student role. Or others in various leadership positions may express explicitly or implicitly that they do not take the role seriously enough, thereby undermining their own work.

- *Role strain:* Some roles can simply be too demanding (in terms of the knowledge or ability they need) for certain people to play them effectively. We might also find ourselves in a role that we are not sufficiently motivated to enact given the unexpected amount of personal investment (in terms of time and energy) it requires.

Whatever the reason for an actor–role mismatch, if it happens it is bad news for the group. Rejected, distorted or only partially enacted roles might upset the whole role system. Ehrman and Dörnyei (1998:147) quote an extract from a student interview that offers a vivid example:

> *The mother-figure girl . . . had enough of always being treated as wise, always being looked upon to provide the answer to our problems, and she rejected this and wanted to get out of this role and, as a matter of fact, this made the group break up.*

7.4 Preparing students for performing their roles effectively

Some students adopt some roles easily and without any obvious effort, but as a general rule, roles usually take more development and learning than we would expect. In order to ensure that students perform their roles effectively, they must receive some explicit preparation. Cohen (1994) recommends that teachers do three things when assigning roles:

- Make the assignment of the roles public so that everybody knows who is 'officially' in charge of what.
- Accompany the roles with specific 'job descriptions'.
- Make sure that everybody is clear about what the role player is supposed to do.

Preparing the students for their roles may take different forms. An initial class discussion with the purpose of raising student awareness about the importance and nature of roles (thereby 'selling the idea') might be the first step, followed by some controlled practice. You may ask students to develop some model scripts, which is particularly useful in language classes, because many roles require special language (see below). Cohen (1994) also recommends that the prescribed behaviours for each role (i.e. the 'job description') are summarised and displayed on a wall chart. This will also 'legitimise' certain things students might need to do in certain roles, particularly in various leadership roles. Finally, after the activity it may be useful – particularly in the early stages – to discuss and reinforce the roles in a wrap-up session.

When assigning roles, we have found it useful after a few minutes to ask all members to report to their groups with regard to their responsibility. Thus, the time-keeper would say how much time is left, the encourager of participation would invite those who hadn't spoken to speak more, and the initiator would report on how they have got started, productively or not. This allows them to practise speaking up and reporting what they are responsible for. The teacher might ask them to do this again near the end of the allotted time to give everyone something to report on and to let them know that in future sessions these roles will be reported on at least twice and should be taken seriously.

The language aspect of performing roles

An important aspect of student roles in language classrooms is the fact that many roles are realised through specific language, often using sets of conventionalised expressions and phrases (just think, for example, of all the fixed phrases we use at a committee meeting). Students will need to perform the various functions in a foreign language, and they are likely to fail to do it well without some explicit initial language input. Thus, when assigning roles, students may find it useful and reassuring to get some tips as to what they might say. These can be small scenarios similar to the following ones:

> OK, my role is to keep everybody on the topic. So I hope you won't mind if occasionally I ask, 'Is what you are saying relevant to our task?' or 'How is that related to what we are trying to do here?'. Or more directly I might point out, 'That doesn't seem to matter, can we go back to the essential things?'

> OK, my role is time-keeper. So I will perhaps interrupt occasionally to let you know how much time we have left. For example, 'Right now, we have spent about 5 minutes of the 30 that we have for the whole task. At this pace we may run out of time.' Or, 'I think we need to move on now to the next stage.' Is this OK with you? But also, I may ask you to decide, 'How much time do we want to spend on this part?' And perhaps I might make an overall time chart for discussion, acting and reflecting,

and see if we can stick to it. I will also remind you that we can change the time settings if we want to. Does that sound OK?

7.5 Self-fulfilling prophecies – or how we live up to the role that is expected of us

Students often come expecting to fill certain roles from their past classes and have certain clear-cut expectations for teachers to fill certain roles as well. In a general sense, if they have mostly been in classes in which teachers only talked at them and students filled the roles of passive listener/test taker, they tend to expect the same. Even though they may not like such roles, many students may grow accustomed to them and fight change. Thus, roles might emerge very much like 'self-fulfilling prophecies': the students live up to – or 'down' to – the expectations that are expressed sometimes blatantly, other times more covertly. For example, a teacher may decide early on that a student will be a trouble-maker. The teacher then acts toward this student as if he expects this behaviour, while in fact it is the teacher who is provoking this behaviour by his or her own behaviour and expectations. With the 'trouble-maker', the teacher might watch carefully for any signs of trouble and, sure enough, find them, even though these signs may be no greater than the indications from other students.

Interesting research: the 'Pygmalion effect'

In one of the most famous experiments is educational psychology, Rosenthal and Jacobson (1968) administered an intelligence test to primary school children at the start of the academic year. Teachers were told that the purpose of this test was to predict which students would 'bloom' intellectually during the academic year. The researchers, however, deceived the teachers because instead of providing them with the true test scores, they identified 20% of the sample as potential 'intellectual bloomers' randomly, that is, regardless of their actual intellectual potential. The results of the experiment were quite remarkable: by the end of the year there were significant differences between the 'bloomers' and the control students whereas at the beginning of the year they were similar in every respect except in the way they were labelled by the researchers.

Although the results of this and follow-up studies have since been subjected to extensive debate, they were useful in highlighting the potential significance of teacher expectations.

The logic of self-fulfilling prophecies suggests that innovative teachers can change student behaviours by making manifest new expectations and generating alternative roles. Granted, students may at first be shocked by the teacher who asks them to take the role of active participant. Helping them become autonomous learners and verbal collaborators may need scaffolding and persistence. A lot may depend on how much the teacher believes students are capable of different roles and behaviours, and how much they make manifest their expectations.

Step into your students' shoes

In order to draw attention to the powerful impact of what might be considered inconsequential teacher comments, we would like to invite you for a brief game. Why don't you step into your students' shoes for a moment and get a feel for what roles are being encouraged by things some teachers may inadvertently say in class. For example, what roles do you think teachers might be inviting or confirming for students with the following communications?

1. 'You are always late and just looking for trouble.'
2. 'You're the last one again. We are forever waiting for you.'
3. 'Your partners tell me that they learn a lot from you.'
4. 'Could you help Emilio with that exercise sheet, please.'

With No. 1, the overgeneralisation of 'always' implies these are part of the student's identity and emphasising it may make the student actually internalise and seek to perform similar acts. With No. 2, the teacher may unknowingly be inviting the rest of the class to view this student as the scapegoat, the problem child, the one who causes us all to slow down and lose time. With No. 3, the teacher is gently suggesting that the student *is* like a teacher and is respected by peers and that the teacher knows this. No. 4 might be a continuation of No. 3 so that the student could more consciously enact the 'helping' role immediately and see how it can become more real and conscious.

To explore this issue further, you might do the following:

1. Record a class and listen to your language.
2. Note what phrases stick out as showing expectations of students (these may be descriptions of the students themselves or of the tasks).
3. Rewrite the ones that might encourage negative roles.
4. Experiment with giving these reformulated communications.

For example, let's say that a teacher actually says Phrase 1 above, 'You are always late and just looking for trouble.' This can be changed to, 'John, sometimes you come late and that disrupts the class. I don't think you mean to be late on purpose, but I just wanted you to know what coming late does to my class [focus on the behaviour not the person]. I was wondering what we [we are in this together] could do about it, because I think you are a good student and I want you to get as much as you can out of the class.'

With practice, re-languaging our communications can become more automatic in the classroom. With more difficult cases, you might try the 'Young Einsteins' fantasy below.

Young Einsteins

I (Tim) once read that Einstein failed French. At about the same time, I also read about self-fulfilling prophecies and I wondered if his failing French happened simply to be the product of teachers who did not expect much from him. Then the thought occurred to me that there might be some Einsteins in my classroom as well. I had a couple of students in my classes at the time that I had labelled 'lost & lackadaisical'. One day in class, instead of ignoring their passivity as I usually did, I put it in my mind that they were both young Einsteins and were going to grow up to amaze the world. When I approached them, I noticed that I did it differently – it was with respect and awe and curiosity that I talked to them. I found out that the boy was a part-time mechanic and fascinated by engines. The girl was a musician in the local orchestra and that was her passion. We talked about these things briefly and I could imagine easily how Einstein's genius would be manifested in their lives. My feelings of awe and respect continued as these two began to open up more and more, first giving me greetings in English and later daring to ask questions in class and then commenting on things they liked and didn't like. After a few weeks they even became passionate about learning English and becoming interactive collaborators with their fellow students. They went from 'lost and lackadaisical' to 'assertive learners' within a month.

This actually scared me when I realised that I might have continued expecting the passivity, and getting it, for the rest of the year. By thinking the opposite, however, I was able to behave differently and inspire a different reaction in my course. Try it sometime. Try believing those 'lost causes' will actually one day be Einsteins. Really believe it when you approach them and your behaviour will be changed. Then just watch what happens.

7.6 'Near peer role modelling'

'Modelling' is held to be one of the most powerful ways of teaching; it involves setting an example that learners find worthy to follow. In a number of writings, Tim has highlighted the potential significance of 'near peer role models' (NPRMs) in language classrooms (Murphey 1995, 1998a, 1998c, 2003; Murphey and Arao 2001). NPRMs are peers who are close to the learners' social, professional and/or age level, and whom the learners may respect and admire. While growing up, many people experience watching some student or sibling just a few years older and modelling their behaviour. In a similar way, if teachers can find productive behaviours, roles and beliefs present in some respectable peer, and highlight these for emulation by others, this can become a powerful means to encourage students to follow the example. During the past decade, Tim has experimented with a variety of ways of highlighting NPRMs. Of these, three in particular lend themselves to modelling role behaviours:

- 'newslettering';
- special topical videos;
- language learning histories.

Yes!

'Seeing or visualising people similar to oneself perform successfully typically raises efficacy beliefs in observers that they themselves possess the capabilities to master comparable activities.'

(Albert Bandura 1997:87)

'Newslettering'

Creating student newsletters entails circulating students' views gathered from their action logs (cf. section 8.1), journals or questionnaires. The newsletters are interesting phenomena because they can provide models of desired, typical or potential roles that students are implicitly invited to take on. And these are *written* descriptions that can be returned to many times and at any time.

Students might read anonymous comments like, 'I used to be silent in class and now I have begun talking more'. They know the comment is from one of their classmates and many of them may identify with the first part (being silent in class); the second part indicates that this peer is changing, which can give them permission to change, too. Thus, the anonymous writer has become a near peer role model.

A newsletter from a third year Taiwanese class is below. Note that the first two comments explicitly address the impact of the newsletters and the modelling of peers through the newsletter:

Student comments from WiZeU Language Lovers Newsletter #6 (*November 2001*)

Newsletter Impact

1. According to the suggestion offered by my classmates [in NL #5], I changed my way of chatting with my partners. This time, I tried to talk to some classmates whom I didn't talk to before. In the beginning, I was afraid of not prolonging the conversation because we were not familiar with each other. Finally, I found I worried too much. They were very easygoing, and it was nice to talk to them. I believe if I can talk to different partners every time, I can get closer relationship with them.

2. I had a bad habit that I would not preview the lesson before the class, because teachers would tell me everything (since elementary school) . . . After reading the newsletter, I thought I had better give up the habit. More and more of my classmates started to push themselves thinking before the teacher telling, and preparing before the teacher asking. That may be the reason why they develop so much.

Speaking English (all I need is 'a little help from my friends')

3. Even after the class, when my friend and I heard someone tell us something embarrassing, we said: 'How embarrassing!' at the same time . . . Through laughter [today] I felt more close to my partners and we can talk to each other with an open mind.

4. I become more familiar with classmates I seldom talk to. Last class, I tried to ask others 'Can I talk with you?' One guy said 'OK'. After talking I find it is happy for me to talk with him. This is a wonderful feeling I didn't have before. So I want to continue to try.

Shadowing

5. Most important of all, when you are telling a story, we all do shadowing. We can imitate the pronunciation and intonation from you.

6. Recently when I watch TV, I avoid watching Chinese captions. I just do shadowing . . . I could learn some practical words, phrases and slang in English . . . it's more interesting than reciting vocabulary one by one.

Notice that the comments in the newsletters do not command or give orders to students, but rather they simply describe possible ways of being in the world. The proximal relationships of the writers and readers, however, invites identification and the realisation that it is possible for the readers to also do the things mentioned in the newsletters. That the newsletters facilitate near peer role modelling is clear from the occasional comments about the newsletters that students make as in the first two in the newsletter above. In the selected quotes below, No. 1 shows students modelling at the level of learning words, expressions and story telling. Nos 2 and 3 comment about identifying similar strategies in others that give one confidence to carry on and to identify with the group. The final two quotes show students who see the newsletters as valuable resources for the class and are more explicitly modelling their peers.

Student comments about the newsletter (from Spring 2002)

1. I'm proud of classmates in the NL [newsletter], because I find many new words or expressions I don't know. By the NL, I can learn other classmates' nice words and expressions . . . Everyone's storytelling is a brand-new impact to my thought and mind, exciting me very much.

2. Because of the newsletter, I realise what my classmates do after the classes. I hope that I can do as well as them!!

3. It's lucky that I saw a classmate wrote that, 'I love the feeling when I talk English to myself.' It feels good that it's not only me that talks to my own self. In English, I love that, too. And I'll keep on doing this.

4. In my mind, newsletter always plays an important role in my learning. When I meet some troubles or difficulties and I feel frustrated, I usually take the newsletters out and read them again, because they encourage me to solve those problems and find the way out . . . They tell me a lot about my classmates' effort and how they do in their daily lives . . . When I feel tired of reading material or writing, I will read newsletters. I love it. It helps me!

5. Every time I see the NL, I can see what my classmates' feeling, sometimes theirs are the same as mine. It gives me lots of encouragement. Also make me eager to learn more. Because they are a very good model for me. Show me what I should do to learn well. Hope one day I can also be a good model for them or someone else.

Topical videos

In the latter half of the 1990s, Tim and his 'Communication Psychology' seminar students at Nanzan University in Japan did a series of quasi-experimental studies involving NPRMs. Kushida (1995) interviewed four enthusiastic students, one at a time, on video and then edited an eight-minute clip which cut quickly from one student to another as they commented on the following ideas:

1. Making mistakes in English is OK.
2. It's good to have goals in learning English.
3. Speaking English is fun.
4. Japanese can become good speakers of English.

Students watching the video identified the four interviewees as near-peers and took on board their views. This video worked so well it has been shown to all first year students in the English department since 1995 (as of this writing in 2002). A more in-depth replication study using the same video was later done (Murphey and Murakami 1998), in which positive results were again attained for students at the same university. Pre- and post-viewing questionnaires showed that students watching the tapes changed their reported beliefs significantly through watching these students talking about taking risks and enjoying English. Later, the video was shown to other university students in Japan and achieved comparable results (Murphey and Arao 2001). Following the success of Kushida's video, a number of similar video projects were carried out under Tim's supervision, focusing on different groups, and the impact was always positive. As a result, we firmly believe that through guided near peer role modelling more students can fill more productive roles in learning communities.

Language learning histories

Each person's *language learning history* is uniquely constructed by events, desires, decisions, strategies, beliefs, actions and particular perceptions. However, we also have many similar characteristics in common with our near peers. We have often gone through the same system, with the same problems, needs and desires. Writing our histories down allows us to reflect on these forces and to become aware of our own part in making our history. And knowing about the choices others have made allows us more choices as well. A history can provide wisdom for the future; multiple histories can provide a vast array of possibilities and potentials. This metacognitive awareness allows us then to take more control of our future learning.

Language learning histories, journals and diaries have become rich tools for many teacher educators and researchers (e.g. Bailey *et al.* 1996; Schumann 1998). They are also excellent material for our students, not only to produce but to read and model, similar to the student newsletters. To allow this, Tim has published several short collections of language learning histories (Murphey 1997, 1998d, 1998e, 1999; see also Oxford & Green 1996). These provide students with intensely relevant and interesting information, level-appropriate reading material, as well as strategies, beliefs and attitudes that can be easily modelled because of the similarities between the writers and readers. While intuitively we realise that younger students might naturally want such stories from their elders, we have found that even older students reading younger students' histories have been impressed and displayed modelling behaviours (Yamashita 1998).

With hopeful expectations . . .

'What is it that one learns by observing peers? We suspect that one learns that certain successes are possible. Learners also find that they can be happy with small successes – they don't have to be frustrated believing that they have to be like native speakers. These learnings give them permission to try certain behaviours with hopeful expectations.'   (Murphey and Arao 2001)

7.7 Summary

In this chapter we have covered the following main points:

- Student roles describe what learners are supposed to do. They can be informal, emerging naturally, and formal, assigned by the teacher.
- Roles are of great importance with regard to the life and productivity of the group. If students are cast in an appropriate role, they will become useful members of the team; however, an inappropriate role can lead to personal conflict and will work against the cohesiveness and effectiveness of the group.
- Teachers can increase the effectiveness and productivity of their classes by inviting or assigning specific student roles. This speeds up the natural process of role division and makes sure that the resulting role pattern best supports the group and suits the task in question.
- In order to ensure that students perform their roles effectively, they must receive some explicit preparation. This may involve teaching

sets of conventionalised L2 expressions and phrases that typically accompany certain roles.

- Near peer role models are peers whom one may respect and admire; highlighting their productive behaviours, roles and beliefs can become a powerful means to encourage students to develop by offering more choices for ways to be in the world.
- Near peer role modelling methods (newsletters, videoing and language learner histories) use the excellence already present in the group to help it become more cohesive and performative.

Important questions about student roles and role modelling

- Which roles do you find among your students or classmates and which ones seem the most problematic for you to deal with?
- What experiences have you had of assigned roles in groups, as a student or as a teacher, and how did it work out?
- What positive and negative effects of student role modelling have you encountered?
- In what ways have you promoted, or could you promote, positive near peer role modelling?

---

8 Trouble-shooting: Conflicts and apathy happen!

This chapter will:

- *discuss why and how conflicts happen in the classroom and what role they play in group life;*
- *present ways of dealing with conflicts of a variety of origins, including conflicts among the students, between the students and the teacher, as well as general class apathy.*

> **Think about it first**
>
> What are the most frequent or biggest conflicts you have had with your students? How are they resolved? What are the conflicts that you worry about most (whether they happen or not)?

Conflicts sometimes happen in the best of learner groups and even with the best of teachers. We know of no colleague who has not had at least a few problems involving confrontations of various sorts, and we suspect that no classes go completely undisturbed. Conflicts happen. We can, however, learn to reduce their number and severity through many of the group dynamic processes outlined in the preceding chapters. We can also anticipate that some will occur, and thus accept or even welcome them, and deal effectively with them to minimise the damage they might cause and maximise their potential for strengthening the interpersonal relationships. It is our belief that to some extent conflicts can be our friends as they help us mature and become stronger as a group.

> **Well said . . .**
>
> 'Most people, if given the choice, avoid situations that are rife with conflict. Yet, conflict is an unavoidable consequence of life in groups. When people are sequestered away from other people, their

ambitions, goals, and perspectives are their own concern. But a group, by its very nature, creates interdependence among its members, raising the possibility that members' likes and dislikes, their opinions and perspectives, their motives and their goals will clash.'   (Donald Forsyth 1999:237–38)

From the teachers' and students' points of view, conflicts can sometimes seem overwhelming. At the extreme, when we have a whole class rebelling against the syllabus, giving up in apathy or fighting interpersonally among themselves, it can seem like we have nowhere to go. And some teachers actually do leave the profession. Much of what we have talked about in the preceding chapters will pre-empt and solve many potential problems by default and lower the magnitude of those that do occur. Time devoted to initial positive group dynamics is like taking immunity shots before travelling – it can make a lot of potentially serious problems unrealisable. But we still might have a few bumps and surprises. In this chapter we will discuss the things we can do that might turn the situation around at times of trouble.

From an interview with a student

I: *Was there anything specific that you didn't like about the class?*
A: *The atmosphere.*
I: *What kind of atmosphere was it?*
A: *That of competition, because the exams generated conflicts amongst us, two different cliques, this kind of thing.*
I: *What kind of conflicts?*
A: *We split up into two different groups and teased each other, laughed at each other in a bad way. When a member of one group started talking the members of the other group tried to find a mistake and raise objections. Generally speaking, there was great rivalry . . . Sometimes the negative atmosphere spread tragically; I mean, insulting expressions.*
I: *How did the teachers react to this kind of behaviour?*
A: *They were tried to quiet us down by talking loudly. Some students were expelled.* (Adapted from Triantafyllopoulou 2002)

8.1 What causes conflict?

Where there is a group, there are bound to be conflicts. What causes these? The sources are numerous and varied; let us mention here the most common ones:

- communication difficulties, misunderstandings and false perceptions;
- disagreements over the way to do tasks or go about things;
- disagreement over rules or policies;
- personality incompatibilities and clashes;
- differences in values, objectives, expectations and motives (including 'hidden agendas');
- unfair or competitive reward allocations;
- scarce resources;
- the leader's inappropriate leadership style, competence or authority.

Furthermore, some conflicts are not caused by anybody in particular but are the natural consequence of the dynamic nature of the group: as we have seen in Chapter 3, the 'storming' period is an inherent part of the 'transition' stage of group development, and – more generally – it has been widely observed that people in general differ in their ability to adapt to change, which will be a source of temporary discord as the group progresses. Finally, some conflicts, such as racial tensions, may be brought into the classroom from the wider environment. Below we look into the main causes in more detail.

Personality conflicts

A common type of classroom conflict involves confrontations among students that are rooted in certain students' antipathy for others. Personal likes and dislikes do not always translate into group conflict because, as we saw in Chapter 1, the group is powerful enough to override initial negative feelings that members may have about each other. In fact, an amazing aspect of group dynamics is that we may like someone in our group that we would not like, or perhaps actively dislike, outside the group! However, some temporary dissatisfaction for another group member is likely to occur from time to time, especially amongst school children, who often go through turbulent periods in their own lives in their maturation process. It is good to remember and to remind students that even friends have conflicts sometimes.

One feature of *personality* or *relationship conflicts* is that although they may be fuelled by underlying disagreements over values, goals, ideas and opinions, as well as by incongruity of personal styles and needs, the actual confrontation may be triggered by a relatively minor disagreement. This then escalates into a negative spiral, with one person's negative comments eliciting equally negative responses from another (Stewart, Manz and Sims 1999), spreading to more affectively loaded areas, with emotional expressions replacing logical discussions. For the outside observer, the whole thing may appear rather childish and insignificant, nothing more than bickering about trivialities, but the expanding negative cycle can be immensely damaging to the group. Breaking the cycle of negative reciprocation is difficult, particularly because, as Ehrman and Dörnyei (1998) argue, many of the reasons for conflict may be unconscious to the members themselves. For example, at the group level, the group as a whole could be avoiding some other form of anxiety by engaging in conflict, either on a broad scale or through 'proxy' members who fight on behalf of the rest of the group.

Well . . .

'Such a cycle of negatively spiralling relationship conflict is often seen as the major cause of failure for perhaps the most common team in existence: a married couple.'
(Greg Stewart, Charles Manz and Henry Sims 1999:96)

Jones and Jones (2000) suggest that teachers be careful about interfering too much in trying to resolve quarrels and rows between students for three reasons:

1. Such conflicts may often be very short-lived, and interference might actually intensify them, particularly when accompanied by punishment.
2. Teacher involvement may also reinforce the undesirable behaviour as students enjoy the attention they get, particularly if it helps to avoid academic work.
3. Excessive teacher involvement in resolving peer conflicts communicates that the teacher does not trust students to resolve them themselves.

We should note, however, that allowing students to work out their conflicts amongst themselves carries the danger of failing to interfere when the situation has turned into a case of bullying and intimidation. We must look out for any signs of this and step in if we feel that a student needs protecting.

Contact helps

It has been our experience that getting students to work together early on during the course can short-circuit a lot of potential personality clashes. When diverse students work on a group task in close proximity, some of the alienating features of the 'other' may be reduced and positive attributes given. Not working together and

---

keeping one's distance tends to augment the suspected 'otherness' as students over-generalise their preconceived notions of the other. Working together can lead students to see different aspects of each other, humanising them in each other's eyes.

Task conflicts

Whereas personality conflicts can be detrimental, task conflicts are more often than not beneficial for the class group. This type of conflict centres not around personality clashes but rather around how certain tasks or projects should be carried out. Issues may involve deciding on the exact procedures to follow, sequencing and timing the various task phases and identifying the exact role of each member in pursuing the executive process. As we will see in section 8.2, a moderate amount of this type of conflict is beneficial because it leads students to critical evaluation of what they should be doing, resulting (hopefully) in increased effectiveness.

Communication conflicts

Some scholars (e.g. Atwater and Bass 1994) believe that of all the conflicts occurring in groups in general, the greatest source is misunderstandings that arise from poor communication among the group members or between the leaders and the members. Insufficient or distorted communication can lead to misconceptions and false perceptions about the motives and goals of others, which is why the main strategy in trouble-shooting in international crises is to initiate talks between the parties at all costs and then try to keep the communication channel open. Fostering an open and accepting climate within the group is half the battle in this respect, and the other half is to air any issue that might cause tension.

Quite so!

'Many conflicts are based on misconceptions. People often assume that others are competing with them, when in fact those other people only wish to cooperate. They think that people who criticise their ideas are criticising them personally. They do not trust other people because they are convinced that their motives are selfish. They assume that their goals are incompatible, when in fact they seek the same outcomes.' (Donald Forsyth 1999:259)

Conflicts associated with group development

Certain conflicts are 'built in' in group development (cf. Chapter 3). The formation of a new group, for example, is characterised by anxiety and personal conflict within each participant about finding the right balance of belonging to the group and maintaining a personal identity. Later in the transition stage, when many of the issues of group formation are on their way to resolution, group members start exploring interpersonal relationships and tasks more deeply. This is when issues of power, control and dominance begin to emerge, resulting in what is often called 'storming'. This, we argued in Chapter 3, is a positive sign that the group is working its way through the process towards cohesiveness.

In addition, most groups display a fluctuation between focusing on its task and productivity on the one hand and the members' psychological needs and group socialisation on the other. It is a bit like a pendulum, and the driving force is the tension and conflicts that arise in the area that is being ignored. Bolstad and Hamblett (1997) assert that for successful groups a 'balancing act' between task and group maintenance needs is required, and that this act may not be easy for many educators.

'Imported' conflicts

Finally, as if the above sources of trouble originating in the classroom group were not enough, some conflicts may actually be 'imported' into the classroom from the wider environment, including racial tensions or conflicts caused by differences in a number of other demographic, socioeconomic or cultural factors such as affluence, class, religion or lifestyle (e.g. rural vs. urban). When these conflicts are dominant in the minds of students and yet remain unaddressed in classes they can greatly disturb learning.

How to keep abreast of what's going on in class: 'Action logging'

With such a diverse range of potential conflicts lurking in the background, it is important for us, teachers, to find a way of keeping abreast of what's going on in class. An effective method of doing so, developed by Tim, is 'action logging' (Murphey 1993; Woo and Murphey 1999). It entails students evaluating the classroom events and reflecting on the usefulness and appropriateness of the activities they have been doing in class in a notebook. The teacher reads the logs weekly, getting feedback on what students liked and what they thought helped them to learn. The teacher can also give feedback personally to individuals. By writing logs, students can review what they have done and feel more involved in the course as they have ongoing communication with the teacher and thus influence the course. Similarly, the action log entries might reveal potential problems and conflicts, helping the teacher to address them in time (Murphey 2001a).

General 'Action Log' instructions for Tim's classes

Get a B5 notebook. At the beginning of every class write at the top of the page the date, your English target to speak (e.g. 80%) and who your partner is. At the end of the class, write how much English you used (e.g. 90%). After every class, as soon as possible (so you remember well what happened), write a short evaluation of the class: (1) List briefly the activities and evaluate them, and (2) write a short comment about what impressed you in that class. Comment on things you liked and could learn from or things you didn't like. Your feedback is needed so that I can teach you better. I read your Action Logs and appreciate your suggestions and will try to use them if possible. You can also draw pictures and take notes in your logs!

Evaluate the activities in three categories, *Interesting*, *Useful* and *Difficult*, marking the extent of each using the following simple scale:

0 = not at all; 1 = not much; 2 = OK; 3 = good;
4 = very good; 5 = great!

An example of an entry:

September 14 (written Sept 14, 21:00)

English Target 75%　　　　　English Used 80% Wow!

Today's partner: Yuki

(1) DID	Interesting	Useful	Difficult
1. listened to a story	4	4	3
2. read a passage	0	1	5
3. discussion	3	3	4
4. teacher lecture	3	4	2
5. had a quiz	2	2	2

(2) **Comment:** I didn't understand some of the points in the reading: What is chunking? Sometimes you spoke too fast. Please speak slower. My partner today was Yuki and it was fun to get to know her. We got a lot of homework, but it looks like fun. I'm looking forward to the next classes. I will prepare more for the quizzes.

If you have anything else that you think the teacher should know (which influenced your learning) please write about it. Please remember two things: (a) Always put the date above the entry and the time when you wrote it in parentheses. (b) Always use people's names when you refer to partners. Leave the Action Logs on the table outside my office door (#000) on _____days. I will return them in the next class. Note that your comments will sometimes be read by your classmates in class (without of course giving your name).

8.2 Potential benefits of conflict

One of the most important messages of this chapter is that, from the point of group dynamics, conflicts are not necessarily bad but can serve a variety of useful purposes – they may be the grist for the mill. We feel that simply being aware of this fact has helped us to cope with them: our first reaction to the occurrence of conflict now is not frustration or disappointment as it used to be but a recognition that the group is moving forward. Indeed, as has been said before (and will be said again), conflicts are useful from the group's point of view because they can provide the necessary push for further development. More specifically, conflicts can be beneficial in at least four important subareas (Wilson 2002):

- *Conflicts can increase student involvement:* We have often found that heated discussions or even confrontations are the sign that the people who were involved in them care, and if the issue in question can be resolved satisfactorily, the parties will be drawn into a deeper commitment.

Indeed . . .

'Heated disagreement can be a good thing in the small group. The emotion and excitement attending a debate can enhance the

> meaningfulness of the subject for the students and can help them to
> remember it.'   (Richard Tiberius 1999:169)

- *Conflicts can provide an outlet for hostility:* By bottling things up, conflicting issues do not go away but fester and might develop into deep-seated hostilities. Giving vent to some of the tension can be liberating provided there is a supportive atmosphere.
- *Conflicts can promote group cohesiveness:* Contrary to beliefs, confrontations do not necessarily ruin the relationship between people but can actually enhance it; Carl Rogers (1970) used the metaphor 'the cracking of facades' to express that even upsetting interpersonal reactions can be constructive as they lead to a deeper and more basic encounter between the parties. You yourself may also have had the experience that after a good fall-out with someone the relationship actually improved.
- *Conflicts can increase group productivity:* Conflict over issues often promotes critical thinking and can help to improve on various task-specific procedures. It would be, in fact, unusual to find a high-achieving group that is not characterised by vibrant disputes that occasionally escalate into rows.

How true . . .

'What is the activator or energy source for transforming the ordinary to the extraordinary? It is the pressure of conflict, the interference patterns of energies caused by differences, that provides the motivation and opportunity for change.'

(Thomas Crum 1987:25)

8.3 Weathering the storm: Conflict resolution

Let us start this section by highlighting what we should *not* do when there is conflict: it is our conviction that in dealing with conflicts we should *not* try to suppress, deny, ignore, minimise or bypass them. We have seen earlier that the group system needs conflict to change and develop. In fact, without any conflict a group is unlikely to be able to develop beyond dependency and superficial forms of acceptance. Accordingly, suppressing conflicts might block group development, and, besides, suppressed conflicts usually leave lingering problems that may resurface later. Thus, our advice is that we should confront conflicts head on and use them to help mature the group. Below, we look at some practical ways to do so.

Reflection

Even though the urge to suppress conflict exists universally, some cultures are more open to disclosing emotions in public than others and therefore confronting conflicts in an open manner is easier in them. What is your culture like in this respect? Can you see any ways of applying what we are suggesting to your home context? Even if you can't, please bear with us – some of the strategies we are going to present might hopefully be adapted in a way that they can work with your students.

Gerald Wilson's (2002:272–74) *list of dysfunctional conflict-management strategies*

- *Do not say, 'Communicate more'* – more of the same sort of communication that has lead to conflict may not be sufficient; what we should also do is communicate *differently*.
- *Do not say, 'Cooperate more'* – people in conflict are usually unable to cooperate on an issue and therefore telling them to cooperate is unhelpful.
- *Do not blame the other person or the group* – being blamed leads to defensiveness, which leads to a rigid position, which leads to poor communication or a return of the blame.
- *Do not attack the other person or persons* – this will only escalate the problem.
- *Do not be too general* – lack of specificity or generalising beyond the current incident makes constructive action difficult; defining the conflict in terms of specific behaviours is a good starting point.
- *Do not avoid conflict* – a strategy of heading off conflict can create resentment and can decrease productivity.
- *Do not try to keep people talking so long that they give up* – the 'it's good to get it all out' strategy often only helps to sustain the conflict indefinitely if it is not accompanied by other, more effective strategies.

These are the 'don'ts'. In the following, we will present numerous effective conflict-management strategies that you can use instead.

When tempers flare – descale the conflict

When tempers flare, the first thing to do is to help students regain control over their emotions (Forsyth 1999). A lot of common-sense practices have been used in schools for years to achieve this. In many conflict situations a cooling-off period, such as an interruption or a break, might provide an opportunity for tempers to subside, and so does the good old 'Count to ten' strategy.

If things get overheated . . .

'If things get overheated or the argument starts to go round in unproductive circles, take a break by asking the group to write instead of speak or playing some music and asking them to close their eyes and relax for a few minutes.'   (Jill Hadfield 1992:159)

Forsyth (1999) also reminds us that an effective way for groups to exercise control over a public display of anger and hostility is to develop norms (cf. Chapter 2) that explicitly prohibit such behaviour. Further-more, it is amazing how much a bit of humour introduced into the situation can help, and learning about mitigating causes that indicate that the insult was not fully, or not at all, intended also help to reduce conflict.

Another useful strategy to descale the conflict is to change the setting from a public to a private one (e.g. your office). Public settings all too often bring 'courtroom drama' where the disputants are playing for the audience rather than focusing on the resolution of the conflict itself. A fight in the playground can often be sorted out better in a quiet room without an audience cheering on the sidelines (Schmuck and Schmuck 2001).

Talk about it!

Our rule of thumb is that conflict situations should not be allowed to fester; they should be brought into the open for discussion and attempted resolution. Not having open communication between students can create a kind of Cold War effect in which each suspects the worst of the other and antagonism and fear grow dangerously inside of each. On the other hand, by actively and openly communicating their motives and reasons, students can undo misunderstandings, false per-ceptions or stereotypes. Open discussion can defuse disputes and bring people together. The teacher's lead in being able to talk calmly and openly about the issues and to show respect for other opinions provides an important model for the students.

A practical technique to initiate discussion that we have used involves students sitting in a circle, everybody completing a sentence stem like 'I feel awful/depressed because . . .'. This technique – labelled as the 'round' by Brandes and Ginnis (1986) – is useful in providing a structure to share feelings and opinions without forcing people to do so (in fact, students are also free to 'pass'). In a safe atmosphere the 'round' can lead to a lively discussion, in which the teacher's role is not so much to give advice or offer solutions as to actively listen to everybody, and then help the group to arrive at a constructive decision about what to do. A well-functioning group that exercises open communication can cope with its problems. With larger classes, this could be done in several smaller groups or in writing (later read by the teacher).

Of course, communication in itself is no cure-all for conflict. Forsyth (1999) reminds us that although communication offers group members the means to undo perceptual misunderstandings and establish trust, it can also create further misunderstandings and deceptions, and it can also 'fan the flames of group dispute' (p. 259).

Tim's secondary school class in Florida

I remember only one teacher in my Florida high school having students talk about the racial riots that were occurring around us in the late 1960s. She dropped the planned literature for two weeks after a local outburst and did nothing but activities concerning interracial understanding. In the other classes, blacks and whites continued to sit separately and to distrust each other. However, she openly addressed the discord by having students form small mixed groups and brainstorm ideas that would ease the tension and resolve some of the problems. These were posted on the wall and the students read them and then wrote essays about the different ideas. We then wrote letters to the local mayor. I remember that class as being the least tense and the one where I was able to concentrate on learning most. Although a lot of difficult feelings remained, when we did go back to learning literature, we did it as a more cohesive group for having addressed our problems first.

Set a superordinate goal

One of the most potent weapons against highly escalated conflict is to set a common, *superordinate goal* for the hostile parties to achieve that requires cooperation. The actual goal can be something like preparing for a sports competition in order to beat the other classes or to participate in an exciting theatre production. Of course, a prerequisite to the effectiveness of this strategy is that the superordinate goal be achieved in the end (Pruitt 1998). Goals that require a division of labour have also been found to be more effective at resolving conflict than those that require the parties to perform the same roles – the latter may lead to competition and unhealthy comparisons.

Interesting research

In his classic book on group conflict, Muzafer Sherif (1966) describes one of the most fascinating experiments in social psychology. In a summer camp in Robbers Cave, Oklahoma, 11 and 12-year-old boys were taken through three main experimental stages. First, they were divided into two groups, the 'Eagles' and the 'Rattlers', and each group was developed into a highly cohesive unit. Then the researchers introduced rivalry between the two groups by means of athletic competition. As a result, the relationship between the two groups deteriorated to such an extent that when, for example, an Eagle was bumped by a Rattler, the fellow Eagles admonished him to brush 'the dirt' off his clothes. There were also fights in the dinner hall. The final part of the project involved reducing the animosity between the two groups. After several ineffective attempts, the researchers decided to promote cooperation by setting a *superordinate goal* which had a compelling appeal for members of each group, but which neither group could achieve without participation of the other. Therefore, they created a series of urgent and natural situations, such as a truck 'breaking down' (the staff had taken care of that), requiring all the children to pull a rope to start it, or the interruption of the camp's water supply, with the boys being asked to search the mile-long water line connecting the camp with a tank. These superordinate goals worked wonders: Eagles and Rattlers stopped shoving each other in the meal line, they no longer called each other names, and they began to sit together at the dinner tables. In the end, they even treated each other to refreshments! The introduction of superordinate goals turned round what appeared a hopelessly divided situation.

Modelling patience

A common source of conflict is when students are impatient or too critical with slower students; this might sow the seeds of greater discontent. Teachers can model patience and compliments for students with slower partners. Pauline Gibbons (2002) describes in detail how teachers can scaffold students' learning and thinking by modelling the behaviour that they want to see in their students. For example, Tim received the comment below from one student that taught him the potential impact of modelling tolerant and inclusive behaviour:

> *At first I didn't want to partner with N. He never says much and it is boring. Then you came to us and you spoke with him slowly. He talked and you said, 'You talk well' to him. He smiled. So I tried to talk slowly like you. Also I say 'you talk well' to him and he smiled. He talked more. I learn more than talk in this class.*

Active listening and the 'summary'

'Active listening', that is, listening respectfully and well, is a greatly under-rated skill, yet it is one that can be very helpful when resolving conflicts. The basic idea is that when a person has a problem or conflict they really need to feel that others are listening to them when they talk. If they don't feel this, the conflict could escalate. Unfortunately, in times of conflict, many people forget to listen well even though listening actively could potentially solve the problem all by itself. What we usually do, instead, is mentally prepare our own counter-arguments while the other person is talking. As a start, we could try and resist leaping in immediately with our own response as soon as the speaker stops, and acknowledge in some way what he or she has said.

The body language of active listening

Bolstad and Hamblett (1997) list the following as helpful in active listening:

- Being close to the person.
- Facing the person and/or leaning towards them.
- Using open body gestures.
- Mirroring the speaker's body posture, breathing and voice-tonality.
- Nodding your head occasionally as they speak.
- Having your eyes facing somewhere near them so they are available for eye contact when they need to be.

- Not doing other things such as gazing out of the window, playing with a pen or reading a book, while the person is talking.

Active listening is more than merely hearing. A good listener displays an attitude of respectful empathy and shows attention through active participation in the form of visual engagement, displayed by such things as eye contact and nodding. A good active listener also gives auditory feedback in the form of partial repetitions of what the speaker says and backchannelling (i.e. giving short 'carry-on feedback' such as 'ah-ha' or 'yeah'), and reflects on content and feeling states ('Oh, that must have hurt'). Bolstad and Hamblett (1997) also suggest making perception checks ('So that made you feel really bad, eh?') and summarising and sorting the issues periodically. Summarising helps a person put the pieces together, both listener and speaker, so they can make better sense of it. Tim has taught language students at all levels to do shadowing (which resembles active, reflective listening) and summarising for over a decade (Murphey 2000) as it makes language more recursive and easier to acquire. Thus, being an active listener serves the double purpose of language learning and effective communication that builds rapport and resolves conflicts.

Tiberius's experience of the 'summary'

'The "summary" is an excellent device for preventing disagreements from degenerating into one-dimensional polemics. Issues are rarely just two sided. A summary enables the group to see the limitations of their statements and to see other dimensions of the argument.

One of the most heated debates I have witnessed was over animal experimentation. Some students were categorically opposed and other were just as rigidly in favour. The commentary had become characterised by slurs and innuendo such as "Nazi mentality" and "anarchists". At this point, the teacher, a small, soft-spoken woman, simply restated the two positions. When the students against animal experimentation heard the sweeping boldness of their statement played back to them they began to make some qualifications about the type of animal . . . The group in favour of experimentation began to qualify what they meant by a "worthwhile" experiment. The debate got unstuck . . .'

(Richard Tiberius 1999:168)

'I' messages

One very frequent feature of confrontations is that when people talk they blame others and tell them they have to change. This, of course, most often elicits resistance and blaming back, and the conflict escalates with a cycle of blaming. Blaming statements usually begin with 'You' and focus on the other person in a highly judgemental and negative way. A simple yet highly effective method of preventing the damage of these 'You messages' is using '*I messages*'. These do not express what we think of another person but rather convey our own feelings and reactions. For example, instead of saying 'You are so irritating when you do this' you might say 'I get irritated when I see that behaviour'. Or, the sentence 'Your idea doesn't make sense' can easily be turned into an 'I sentence': 'I can't make sense out of that idea.' 'I messages' are especially disarming because we admit to our own problem ownership and we are not attacking another, thereby creating a bigger conflict.

Elisabeth Cohen (1994) goes one step further and suggests that blaming sentences should not be turned merely into 'I statements' but rather into 'I feel' statements, in which students express honestly how they felt in response to the other person's statement or behaviour. For example, the sentence 'You told me my ideas stink' can be translated into 'When you told me my ideas stunk, I felt like no one in this room wanted to hear anything I had to say'. This would open the path for explanations and qualifications.

'I messages' do not usually solve everything, but they do make the communication go smoother and clarify things for the parties involved. We must also add at this point that it is very easy to drift into blaming language in times of conflict and it takes practice to stay in the 'I' mode, particularly because this is not a natural way for most people to talk.

Student practice exercise of 'I feel' statements developed by Diane Kepner

'"I feel" statements focus on our own feelings in response to the other person's behaviour. They consist of three parts: identifying the behaviour, expressing the feelings experienced as a result of the behaviour, and explaining the reasons for those feelings. A useful formula for phrasing "I feel" statements is:

When you . . . (State problem behaviour)
I feel . . . (Express feeling)
Because . . . (State reasons for your feeling)

Share with the class the following examples of "You" statements and contrast them with "I feel" statements related to the same

---

topic. The examples are all taken from common conflicts in small groups. Have a small group of students come up and act out the two alternative responses. Have the class analyse the "I feel" statements in terms of the formula. Can they construct alternative "I feel" statements that fit the formula? You can use buzz groups for this exercise.

Situation 1: A member of your group interrupts you constantly when you are talking.

"You" statement: "You're so rude! You never let me say anything!"

"I feel" statement: "When you interrupt me, I feel really hurt because I think that what I have to say is important too."

Situation 2: Two members of the group are holding the task cards so that you can't see the diagrams.

"You" statement: "You guys are always hogging everything!"

"I feel" statement: "I feel left out when you guys have the cards between you because I can't follow what's going on."

Situation 3: A member of your group is busy shooting paper wads at someone in another group and talking to members of the other group.

"You" statement: "You're such a goof-off. You never help!"

"I feel" statement: "When you start doing things with people in other groups I feel really upset because we need everyone's help to get this project done on time."' (Cohen 1994:180–81)

Dealing with problem students

From time to time, students will engage in disruptive behaviour that may be independent of the group process and is caused by some individual psychological need. McCombs and Pope (1994) argue that, contrary to belief, most misbehaviour in the classroom is the result of the students' low self-esteem: 'Students, rather than being malicious, attention-seeking egomaniacs, are misbehaving because they're scared or insecure' (p. 40).

As we said in Chapter 2, in well functioning and cohesive groups, the teacher can often count on considerable peer pressure to stop the 'sabotage'. In such groups, as Brandes and Ginnis (1986:41) summarise, 'the burden of discipline has been lifted from the teacher and placed where it belongs, on each person present. In this way all behaviour problems become group problems'. It may be sufficient for the teacher handling such conflicts to *remind* people of the ground rules. With maturity and time, the group can reach a point where they are capable of renegotiating the rules and agreements.

Unfortunately, there will be times when the group won't do the job for us and we must confront students about misbehaviour. At times like this, the rule of thumb generally mentioned in the literature is that we should address the issue directly, trying to discuss with the students involved what they can do to engage in more positive behaviour. This may be easier if we manage to separate students from their actions in the spirit of 'I accept you but not your behaviour'. We should also remember that 'congruence' was described in Chapter 6 as a positive feature of the teacher-facilitator. So we can be congruent at times of trouble as well, and express how angry or frustrated we are about the disruption.

Three key reasons to avoid confrontational behaviour management

1. It doesn't work.
2. If we use it, it not only models it but legitimises our students using it.
3. It damages self-esteem and many of your students will be vulnerable already in this area.

(Peter Hook and Andy Vass 2000:68)

Skeleton of assertive behaviour to deal with problem-students

1. State your point of request.
2. Actively listen to the other person's viewpoint, reflecting back the essence of what is said without comment or criticism, thus acknowledging that you understand their point.
3. Calmly restate your point of view or request.
4. Actively listen as before.
5. Restate your position.

And so on . . .

As Brandes and Ginnis (1986:42) argue, such a 'broken record' technique is effective because the other person has been listened to and valued (something that does not often happen in arguments) and can therefore concede a point without losing face.

Mediating conflicts

Ideally, conflict between individuals or groups is best resolved directly by the opposing parties themselves. Teachers can facilitate this by bringing the disputants together and encouraging them to work things out. Schmuck and Schmuck (2001) point out that the 'Come and see me when you have reached an agreement' instruction is quite often sufficient to achieve peace. However, when the communication skills of the students who are involved in the confrontation are lacking or because the animosity is so great that it prevents constructive inter-action, teachers may step in as a third party to act as a *mediator*. This role is very different from being an arbitrator or a judge because mediators do not make any decisions or settle disagreements; they only assist the progress of reconciliation by performing a number of impor-tant functions (Forsyth 1999):

- Regulating turn-taking so that both sides are given an opportunity to express themselves.
- Clarifying issues if the two disputants begin to misunderstand each other.
- Helping the parties to save face by providing a graceful means of accepting compromises.
- Offering proposals for alternative solutions that both parties find acceptable.
- Manipulating aspects of the meeting, including its location, seating, formality of communication and time constraints.
- Guiding the disputants through the process of problem solving.

An important aspect of mediation is to make the two parties talk to each other by asking, for example,

- to describe what happened and how they feel;
- to paraphrase the *other's* position and how the *other* feels;
- to tell each other what they can do to avoid the conflict in the future;
- to search for a solution, going back and forth between the parties;
- to repeat the solution they have found and agreed on by both parties.

It might be useful at each step to ask each party to restate the other's position in order to clear up any discrepancies in what one party said and another heard.

The important thing about mediation is to provide the parties with an adequate structure to follow. Jones and Jones (2000) report that in some American classes, *worksheets* have been used successfully to help students structure the meeting and report their solution. These work-sheets identify the behaviour that has triggered the quarrel, examine the quarrel's effect and whether it has involved the violation of any class-room norms, and require completion of the following two sentences: '*We have decided that we will . . .*' and '*The next time one of us does something that bothers the other, we will . . .*'. The form is then signed by the conflicting parties.

Whatever gave you this idea?

'It may happen, though, that your best attempts to resolve the crisis fail and the group cannot be reconciled. In this case . . . you may feel guilty, inadequate, or demoralised: somehow as teachers we have the feeling that we *ought* to be able to resolve all human conflict, and if we meet a problem that defies our best efforts to solve it we have failed in our job. Whatever gave us this idea?'

(Jill Hadfield 1992:157)

8.4 Rebellion against the leader

Although blatant and full-scale rebellion is not that common in most school environments in the world, it does happen sometimes, particularly in more subtle forms (and as we gather from the media, its frequency is on the increase). Manifestations of rebellious attitudes can range from openly speaking up and questioning decisions, rules or practices, to a variety of less obvious and obliquely corrosive ways, such as avoidance (lateness, poor attendance), gradual withdrawal of motivation, passive aggression and so on. Ehrman and Dörnyei (1998) argue that teachers often adopt a controlling and suppressive approach in such situations, because they feel threatened by them and do not recognise this as a stage in the development of a mature, interdependent group. This is understandable, since being on the receiving side of corporate student challenges or hostility *is* scary and unnerving. And, as Richard Tiberius (1999), a highly experienced educational trouble-shooter, has concluded, one of the most common fears teachers have disclosed to him over the years is the fear of losing their authority. Yet, bearing in mind the following two points might be helpful to weather the storm:

- It is a well-documented and natural characteristic of group development that feelings of *emotional closeness* and *separateness* of the members fluctuate (Shambaugh 1978). During periods of closeness and solidarity, the general emotion underlying group interaction is the desire for intimacy and acceptance, and the group leader is seen as benevolent. However, during phases of emotional distance, the underlying emotional issues are hostile, competitive impulses, and the leader is perceived as exploitative and manipulative. The good news is that, with the group's development, the group structure becomes more solid, the intensity of the emotional fluctuation decreases and affective energies tend to be channelled into the tasks (cf. Chapter 3 on group development).

- The suppression of this kind of rebellion is counterproductive. Although aggression that is aimed at the teacher might be kept at bay, this may result in it being displaced onto the subject matter, the institution or selected scapegoats. Indeed, an increase of bullying and school violence may often be the result of the perceived failure for students to have their voices heard and, more generally, to exercise some control in their classes and in their lives (Yoneyama 1999).

In view of the above, we believe that there is a strong case for looking at student rebellion as the first significant step towards student autonomy, which is a welcome sign in group development. We also believe that if teachers succeed in handling such challenges in a sensitive, open and non-defensive manner, this may bring the teacher–student relationship to a new level of maturity. It's a bit like giving vent to hostile reactions in intermember conflicts: they often result in a deeper level of understanding and acceptance between the opposing parties. Of course, it is easy to lose patience with the students' lack of respect for us but if there is a way, we should resist an appeal to authority. On the other hand, we also believe that the teacher has both the right and the obligation to insist on civility while riding out a group's rebellion phase (Ehrman and Dörnyei 1998).

> *Yes!*
>
> 'Of course, it's no fun to teach students who are ridiculing or heckling you. But, short of that kind of rudeness from students, my view is that we should welcome any attempt from students to take over the authority and responsibility for the course. After all, learning is the purpose of the entire effort. We teachers are helpers. The more teaching the students take over, the easier our job and, often, the better the learning becomes.' (Richard Tiberius 1999:166)

8.5 When apathy sets in

There are times when all or most of the students just seem 'tuned out': they look bored or sleepy, their attention drifts and they don't want to do anything. All your efforts to stir them up bounce back as if from a brick wall. In short, there is a general student apathy. What should we do in such situations (apart from screaming 'Help!')?

When the class has 'gone off the boil'

'Unfortunately, classes which have become bonded do not always remain so. A number of teachers experienced classes which had "gone off the boil", and knew that when this happened they needed to take urgent action in order to rekindle interest and propel the class forward in a new direction. In terms of group dynamics a number of tactics are available. These include renegotiating goals, by inviting student suggestions for a new language focus, new topics, new themes, or new activities. Fresh activities, such as a class outing or a class party, can help the teacher to see students in new roles, especially when the students themselves have organised the event. Teachers can often have ideas for a new focus from chance remarks of behaviours of individual students, and can get students to adopt new group enhancing roles for the remainder of the course.' (Rose Senior 1997:10)

When apathy sets in, what we have on our hands is a motivational problem – the students have lost interest. Accordingly, what we need to do is *motivate* them. Zoltán's summary of motivational strategies (Dörnyei 2001a, 2001b) offers a variety of techniques that are available for language teachers. Discussing these in detail would go beyond the scope of this book, so we will only address one particularly relevant issue, promoting the group's *goal-orientedness*. In the table below we have listed a selection of other strategies that can be used to remedy apathy.

Motivational strategies from Dörnyei's (2001b) list to combat apathy

Make learning more stimulating and enjoyable by breaking the monotony of classroom events:
- Vary the learning tasks and other aspects of your teaching as much as you can.
- Occasionally do the unexpected.

Make learning stimulating and enjoyable for the learner by increasing the attractiveness of the tasks:
- Make tasks challenging.

- Make task content attractive by adapting it to the students' natural interests or by including novel, intriguing, exotic, humorous, competitive or fantasy elements.
- Personalise learning tasks.
- Select tasks that yield tangible, finished products.

Make learning stimulating and enjoyable for the learners by enlisting them as active task participants:
- Select tasks which require mental and/or bodily involvement from each participant.
- Create specific roles and personalised assignments for everybody.

Present and administer tasks in a motivating way:
- Explain the purpose and utility of a task.
- Whet the students' anticipation about the content of the task.
- Provide appropriate strategies to carry out the task.

Provide learners with regular experiences of success:
- Provide multiple opportunities for success in the language class.
- Adjust the difficulty level of tasks to the students' abilities and counterbalance demanding tasks with manageable ones.
- Design tests that focus on what learners can rather than cannot do, and also include improvement options.

Increase learner satisfaction:
- Monitor student accomplishments and progress, and take time to celebrate any victory.
- Make student progress tangible by encouraging the production of visual records and arranging regular events.
- Regularly include tasks that involve the public display of the students' skills.

Promoting the group's goal-orientedness

The group's *goal-orientedness* refers to the extent to which the group is attuned to pursuing its goal (in our case, L2 learning). We are in complete agreement with Hadfield (1992:134) when she emphasises that, 'It is fundamental to the successful working of a group to have a sense of direction and a common purpose. Defining and agreeing on aims is one of the hardest tasks that the group has to undertake together'. Whereas in the 'real world' groups are often self-formed for a voluntarily chosen purpose, in school contexts the overwhelming majority of classes are formed for a purpose decided by outsiders – policy and curriculum-makers. Thus, the 'official group goal' (mastering the course content) may well not be the only group goal and in extreme cases may not be a group goal at all; furthermore, members may not show the same degree of commitment to the group goal. Indeed, we have found that when participants of a new course shared openly their *own* personal goals, this has usually revealed considerable differences.

In the light of this, Dörnyei and Malderez (1999) find it particularly important that the group agree on its goal by taking into account *individual goals* (which may range from having fun to passing the exam or to getting the minimum grade level required for survival) and *institutional constraints* ('You're here to learn the L2, this is the syllabus for this year!'), as well as the *success criteria*. Traditionally, these latter have been to do with exams and marks, but other communicative criteria can often be a better incentive, for example to be able to understand most of the words of the songs of a pop group, or other specific communicative objectives. In response to these considerations, Zoltán has formulated the following goal-related motivational strategies (Dörnyei, 2001b):

- Increase your students' goal-orientedness by formulating explicit class goals accepted by them:
    Have the students negotiate their individual goals and outline a common purpose, and display the final outcome in public.
    Draw attention from time to time to the class goals and how particular activities help to attain them.
    Keep the class goals achievable by re-negotiating if necessary.
- Use goal-setting methods in your classroom:
    Encourage learners to select specific, short-term goals for themselves.
    Emphasise goal completion deadlines and offer ongoing feedback.
- Use contracting methods with your students to formalise their goal commitments:
    Draw up a detailed written agreement with individual students, or whole groups, that specifies what they will learn and how, and the ways in which you will help and reward them.
    Monitor student progress and make sure that the details of the contract are observed by both parties.

8.6 Summary

In this chapter we have covered the following main points:

- Conflict is natural and inevitable in human relations; it has multiple origins.
- Conflict can have several positive functions in the life of a group.

- Effective group-building strategies early in a group's life make conflict less frequent and less trenchant.
- A wide array of strategies to handle conflict effectively and to teach the students to deal with it are available.
- Teachers need not panic when there are conflicts or low points. Very often these are natural concomitants of group life that every healthy group undergoes.
- Most conflicts can be dealt with openly (and of course sensitively) – suppressing them will usually not make them go away.
- We should have enough trust in our group to assume that it can cope with its problems. The teacher doesn't have to always *solve* them, but rather bring them up for discussion.
- Some apathy may occur in any group in the cycle of their learning: people get tired and may change priorities. Increasing goal-orientedness and applying other motivational strategies may be effective in livening up the class group.

A parting plea

'Conflict is generally uncomfortable and tension producing, which is why people avoid it if possible. Problems that produce this high level of tension are not likely to go away on their own. Confronting the differences usually produces beneficial results. [Muster] the courage to confront the differences that affect your group.'

(Gerald Wilson 2002:287)

Important questions about classroom conflicts

- What stories of conflict in groups could you share with colleagues? What have your personal reactions been to conflict in the groups you have participated in?
- What positive and negative resolutions to conflict have you experienced?
- How have you personally handled conflict effectively in the past?
- How comfortable are you at remaining patient and letting conflict run its course?
- What conflict situations are you in, or potentially in, right now and how might they be resolved?
- What advice would you give to a new teacher who was experiencing apathy in classes?

9 The last classes: Affirming and closing

This chapter will describe the importance of the teacher guiding students to:

- *affirm what they have learned and achieved;*
- *bring appropriate emotional closure to a course;*
- *project into the future;*
- *provide valuable feedback on the course for the teacher's professional development.*

> **Think about it first**
>
> As a teacher, what do you usually do during the last class to say goodbye to your students? Do you remember any of your teachers closing particularly well when you were a student?

The following is a re-creation of a teacher's speech in the last class of an adult language course, after reviewing the things learned and singing a song together:

> Today is the last class. I'm going to pass out a feedback form now. I would like you to fill it out for me so that I can improve the course in the future. Before I do, I just want to say that I have enjoyed being with you in the class. And I've enjoyed watching how you learned and progressed. The class is over – however, I hope you will continue to study and to learn. I would enjoy hearing from you later if you wish to contact me and tell me about the wonderful things you are doing with your life. I hope also that I will see you in other courses later. Thank you very much for your energetic participation. Good luck.

The forms are passed out. The teacher turns on some background music while students fill them out. Students file out one by one, or in twos and threes, many stopping to say a personal goodbye to the teacher or talking to others just outside the door.

What do you think? Is this how a group should end? Is this what the students and the teacher needed? In general, how do we close well? In this chapter we address these questions. In our view the dissolution stage of group development is very important, and yet we find that this stage is all too often ignored or played down by teachers.

9.1 The significance of an appropriate closure of the group

The final phase of group development is the *dissolution stage* (cf. Chapter 3). This can be planned or spontaneous. Planned dissolution takes place when the group accomplishes its prescribed goals or when the scheduled time of its existence expires. This is, for example, the case with an *ad hoc* school committee and with virtually all language classes. Spontaneous dissolution is much less frequent in education; it happens when an unexpected event, problem or external decision leads to the disbanding of the group or if the group fails to satisfy its members' needs and they decide to abandon it *en masse* and join other organisations (Forsyth 1999).

In any case, groups end – this is inevitable. So why not simply say goodbye and get on with our lives? Why make a fuss? Or do we need to make a fuss? The answer to this last question is 'Yes', for at least three reasons:

- An appropriate closure offers opportunities for a great deal of teaching/learning and motivating to take place that would be missed out on if we did not include some affirmation of what has been achieved.
- Leaving the group without proper closure on personal, emotional issues can cause considerable unprocessed distress in the group members.
- An inappropriate closure might leave students without any specific action plans as to how to carry on outside the group in the future.

As we pointed out in Chapter 3, not every class group goes through the group development process. Very large lecture courses, for example, experience few of the stages that we have described in the preceding chapters, and even some smaller classes may never become more than a group of 'tourists' momentarily coming together to do individual tasks with little investment in relationships with others. In these cases the closing functions associated with the dissolution of the group can be covered relatively quickly. However, language classes, in contrast to most other kinds of learner groups, tend to experience much more interpersonal and group processes. Ehrman and Dörnyei (1998) list two reasons for this:

- Language classes are usually relatively small (even a class of 30 cannot compare with a lecture section of 100).
- Current teaching theory and practice promote active communication among the members (although in traditional settings this may not be so and the language class might be as uncommunicative as any other). By the nature of the communicative language teaching activities, like icebreakers, role plays, pair and group work or field trips, class members come to know one another and group development tends to take place whether attended to or not.

This being the case, language classes are often characterised by a relatively advanced stage of group development, which highlights the need for rounding up the group experiences appropriately.

In short . . .

'Closing is about acknowledging the past and setting a course for the future, while celebrating the moment.'

(Tim Kemp and Alan Taylor 1992:26)

9.2 Affirming and motivating

To affirm means to validate, strengthen, support and renew – something that is clearly relevant to what has been learned and, more generally, what has been achieved during the course. One of the key functions of closure is reaffirming the group's progress in learning and also in other areas. This can be done by summarising and evaluating what the students have accomplished, pulling together loose ends to show how the course was coherent, and rounding off things in a positive and forward-looking way. This is the time to feel empowered by the learning that has taken place, while feeling confident that the skills and knowledge attained will be of particular use. This is also the time to celebrate.

Teachers often assume that students already know all that they have done during the term or course and thus to talk about it any more would be overkill. However, it is the moment at the top of a mountain after a hard climb that every climber loves most. They want to cherish that view and look back at what they have accomplished. It is only at times of taking stock of past achievements that learners realise just how much they have done and how far they have gone.

Closure is not a one-off event but a gradual process intensifying in the last few classes. We advise starting to do many of the activities connected with the end of group life a few weeks before it actually happens to allow students to feel the end coming and to adjust to it incrementally rather than all at once. Signalling that the end is approaching can be done in a variety of ways. Teachers can begin by reminding students gently, 'Unbelievable – we only have four classes left.' This can be followed by guiding the class through a revision of the instructional material. The teacher can also start recalling stories of some 'magic moments' or of various group members doing different things during the course, and encourage learners to do the same. Some teachers like questionnaires that list the activities that have been done and ask students to rate these so that the teacher can change and teach better the next time (for more about this, see section 9.5). Besides serving as useful feedback, these evaluations provide the group with the opportunity to acknowledge just how far they have moved.

Another option is to ask students to write a short report of the course and what they have learned to bring to the last class to share with their classmates and to turn in to the teacher. Other teachers might ask for a self-evaluation by the students that pushes them to assess what was done and how they participated in the course. When self-evaluation forms are used for grading, these can be given out at the beginning of the course as well as the end so that students can project from the beginning what activities they will be doing and know how they will be evaluated.

Tim regularly videoes students having conversations in his conversation classes and asks them to compare their first and last conversations in a report. They attach copies of their transcriptions, with numbered lines, and write about how they have changed. They already know they are going to do this at the beginning of the term and can project how they want to be different. The writing of the report is an effective way of looking back and seeing where they were and how far they have come. Below is an example of the beginning of a such a paper from Melody:

MY FINAL PAPER IN VIDEO CLASS

First of all, I felt a little upset while writing the final paper. It meant that I have finished my video class and I couldn't enjoy this class again. I really had much fun and learned many interesting things from what you have taught us. I could talk about amusing topics in English and record my conversation with different partners. I have become accustomed to speaking English not only in class but also in

---

my daily life. I am willing to talk in English and it is easy to find partners who are willing to talk with me. Furthermore, I feel much more confident of speaking bravely and showing my thoughts exactly. It is also the most important part for me because confidence can encourage me to learn what I was afraid of. Therefore, I know I have improved a lot in many aspects.

The following are some reasons for my improvement in video recording this semester. First, in Transcript One, lines . . . (etc.)

The point behind all these methods is that they get students to think back and have a look at where they have been and where they are now. Parties, graduations, speeches and exchanges of small gifts also acknowledge the end and celebrate accomplishment. All this obviously has a significant learning and consolidation effect but this is not the whole picture. It is a characteristic of human nature that we spend a great deal of our time looking back, evaluating what we have done and how well it went. This retrospection will then lead to lessons drawn for times to come, and in this way the past becomes closely tied to the future. What makes this an important consideration for group dynamics is that this retrospective human evaluation is rather *subjective*: students' appraisal of their past performance does not only depend on the absolute level of success they have achieved but also on *how* they interpret their achievement. Therefore, an appropriate closure that helps to put things in a positive light plays a very important role in motivating students to pursue further academic achievements, and will also have a considerable impact on their future approach to learning in groups in general.

Thus, a key aspect of the dissolution stage involves helping students to deal with their past in a way that will promote rather than hinder future efforts. Recognising what the group and its members have accomplished will give the positive experiences a chance to be transferred to the students' lives away from the class.

Feedback activity: The string toss game

This game gives a structured opportunity for students and teachers to realise the emotional ties amongst themselves and to share some positive feelings by giving others in the group a compliment or word of thanks. The activity also has a symbolic significance in that the string that is first used to link each member of the group is cut in the end.

A ball of string and scissors are required. The group needs to sit in a circle. The teacher begins the activity by throwing the ball of string – making sure that he/she holds on to one end – to a student of the group and giving some positive feedback to the person about their part in the group. That person will then throw the ball of string to another member of the group, again making sure that he or she keeps hold of the string, and gives the person they threw the string to positive feedback and so forth.

An alternative is to make the activity less structured by inviting volunteers to say goodbye to the group by telling them about a special memory they have of the class, what they have learned, or what they feel at the moment. In this version, the teacher would begin by saying a few words and then a student would volunteer to go next and the teacher would throw the ball to them while holding onto the end, and so forth.

This continues until the string crosses back and forth across the room and everyone has spoken and the ball of string returns to the teacher. The teacher then cuts the end from the ball and ties the two ends together. The teacher remarks something to the effect that:

> We are all connected, like this string that we are holding now. We have been influenced by each other and learned a lot. However, soon we will be parting and this string is just a reminder that we have connected and made friends and left impressions on each other. When one person in this group pulls on their string, it effects all of us. That has been our class experience. I would like to offer you a part of this string to take with you as a memory of the things you have done here, the friends you have made, the learning you have done. I am going to cut the string now in the middle, between each of you. Please hold on to your part. Some people might tie their string above their desks, some keep it for a while in their purses. Eventually most people will lose their pieces of string and that is OK. But when you see other pieces of string, you may still think of the ties you have made in this group and in other groups. Again thank you very much for your participation.

(This is a popular activity published in several versions. See, for example, Kemp and Taylor 1992:109–10; Kindt 2001:39.)

9.3 Emotional closure

Psychologists call it 'separation anxiety'. It swells unavoidably the closer we get to the end of a course. It concerns the stressful dynamics evoked by the imminent ending of the group. Members mourn for the group; they experience a feeling of emptiness and loss. No matter what the lasting rewards of the group experience are, when the group comes to an end, it hurts. The sadness may be unconscious and expressed through defensive behaviour like denial ('This isn't adieu; it's au revoir') or avoidance ('No, I won't really miss it. I'm too busy doing other things') (Ehrman and Dörnyei 1998).

Thus, the closure of a group is also important to the emotional life of its members and when ended positively it will affect how students relate to new groups. If the inevitable sadness is not acknowledged and dealt with, there is a danger that it can slip the group members back into defensiveness. The teacher's job at this stage is to get the group to accept that the end is coming and to let members know how it will be handled. It is important that teachers structure activities that help students to say goodbye gracefully. The teacher can take the lead in modelling the expression of regret at leaving and the hopes for further contact in the future.

Parting can be painful, yet it is this pain that confirms that participants have bonded and formed worthwhile relationships. 'No pain, no gain' is true at the time of group dissolution.

Feedback activity: Talking wall

This activity helps group members to generate and share reflections and observations about the group and the course. You will need sheets of flip chart paper, each headed with a topic of relevance to the group/course: 'Things I enjoyed', 'Things that made me laugh', 'What I got from the course', 'What I intend to do next', etc. Put these on the walls all around the classroom.

Now ask everybody to note down their thoughts or comments for each heading on 'Post It' notes or simply on a piece of paper. They are welcome to prepare as many slips as they wish. After sufficient time has been given, ask the group to stick their comments on the appropriate pieces of flip paper (or they can also simply write their comments on the charts). When this has been done, encourage students to move around the room, reading what others have said.

You can add the follow-up task that while students are reading each other's views, they should mark each comment with a tick or a cross to indicate agreement or dissension.

(Tim Kemp and Alan Taylor, 1992)

9.4 Projecting into the future

'Closing' is not simply saying goodbye. It is in a very real sense a beginning for a new phase for the students: the 'life after the group'. The final aspect of the teacher's role, then, is to prepare the participants for re-entering the world outside the group. There are at least three points to cover:

- Language learning is a life-long activity, and therefore students will appreciate any advice about how to carry on learning or how to maintain their acquired proficiency. This is the time to identify new targets, to recommend further materials and resources, and to discuss the possibility of students' joining another group. In an ideal situation, students leave a course with a plan of action about their next steps. Conversation activities which ask, 'What will you do in the next few weeks or months after the course?' might be particularly useful in this respect.
- Some members might need special attention because they have specific plans after the course, such as travel or special exams.
- Members will often want to find ways of keeping in touch. Teachers can facilitate this by organising address lists and follow-up/reunion parties. When ongoing contact is relatively easy, as in a school or university, some groups may continue to meet in whole or in part, postponing final closure. Such meetings usually depend most on proximity of the members and the energy of one or two people who want to keep the group and its good experience alive. Sooner or later even these enthusiasts realise it is time to move on.

Absolutely!

'It is important to give students some sense of continuity after the abrupt end of a course that may have been a major part of their lives for some three months, or even longer. Two areas are important here: keeping up the English they have learned, and keeping up the friendships they have made.' (Jill Hadfield 1992:163)

9.5 The teacher-leader's needs

Closing the group would not be complete without the teachers taking care of their own needs. Most important of these is to seek feedback from the learners in order to evaluate the course design and their own performance within it so that they can change and teach better the next time. Many institutions make such student evaluations obligatory, but very often the questions are geared at obtaining some overall ratings (which the institution needs) rather than covering specific aspects of the course (which the teacher would need). A feedback form used by Tim is presented in the box below, and for more information on how to construct questionnaires, please refer to Zoltán's recent book *Questionnaires in Second Language Research* (Dörnyei 2003).

Finally, as group leader, do you feel able to acknowledge your own learning after a course?

Feedback form used by Tim in a course in 1997

Please help me to teach better. Let me know if you enjoyed the following components of your course and how useful they were. Do not put your name on this form. Just circle the numbers (1 = not at all . . . 5 = completely).

For example, if you thought the book was somewhat enjoyable and useful, you might circle '3' under ENJOYABLE and '4' under USEFUL. If you thought the text was NOT enjoyable or useful you might circle 2. If you didn't do an item and have no information, please leave it blank.

	ENJOYABLE	USEFUL
1. Main class text	1 2 3 4 5	1 2 3 4 5
2. Additional articles/handouts	1 2 3 4 5	1 2 3 4 5
3. Juggling	1 2 3 4 5	1 2 3 4 5
4. Songs	1 2 3 4 5	1 2 3 4 5
5. Background music	1 2 3 4 5	1 2 3 4 5
6. Stories	1 2 3 4 5	1 2 3 4 5
7. Re-telling stories (reformulation)	1 2 3 4 5	1 2 3 4 5
8. Writing the Action Log	1 2 3 4 5	1 2 3 4 5
9. Home/assignment: meeting with classmates	1 2 3 4 5	1 2 3 4 5
10. Telephoning assignment	1 2 3 4 5	1 2 3 4 5
11. Changing partners	1 2 3 4 5	1 2 3 4 5
12. The balance of theory and practice	1 2 3 4 5	1 2 3 4 5
13. Teacher's classroom organisation	1 2 3 4 5	1 2 3 4 5
14. Teacher's blackboard work	1 2 3 4 5	1 2 3 4 5

	ENJOYABLE					USEFUL				
15. Teacher's explanations in class	1	2	3	4	5	1	2	3	4	5
16. Teacher's comment in your logs	1	2	3	4	5	1	2	3	4	5
17. Teacher's use of Japanese in class	1	2	3	4	5	1	2	3	4	5
18. Content of the course in general	1	2	3	4	5	1	2	3	4	5
19. Shadowing	1	2	3	4	5	1	2	3	4	5
20. Learning from classmates	1	2	3	4	5	1	2	3	4	5
21. Helping classmates to learn	1	2	3	4	5	1	2	3	4	5
22. Paper one	1	2	3	4	5	1	2	3	4	5
23. Paper two	1	2	3	4	5	1	2	3	4	5
24. Mid-term test	1	2	3	4	5	1	2	3	4	5
25. Self-evaluation	1	2	3	4	5	1	2	3	4	5

Please comment in writing on any of these that you wish to. You can use the back.

Thank you!

9.6 Summary

In this chapter we have covered the following main points:

- An appropriately conscious closure affects students' present state and future learning.
- Affirming and highlighting what has gone on in the class serves an important instructional function and it also helps to leave a positive impression of the group experience, thereby motivating students to join new groups and seek new experiences later.
- Teachers can attend to the swelling of separation anxiety and create healthy emotional closure by allowing and encouraging the open expressions of students' feelings.
- Projecting into the future will help students think about life after the group and be prepared for living beyond the group.
- The teacher's requests for student feedback about the course can serve the double purpose of preparing closure and providing valuable information to the teacher for professional development.

Important questions about closure

- What good and not so good last goodbyes do you remember in the groups you have belonged to? What made them good and memorable, or not so good?
- What stories do you have of experiences of separation anxiety? Under what conditions did they occur and how did they end?
- Are there any closing functions that you have not regularly included in your teaching? What kind of goodbye class do you think would be ideal for the course(s) you teach now?
- What kind of feedback from students have you found useful at the end of the course and what kinds not? How can we get more of the first?
- Have you been to any reunion parties during the past few years? If so, were they what you expected? If not, why not?

10 Conclusion: Wrapping it up

In the *Afterword* of the book that Zoltán wrote with Madeline Ehrman on group psychology (Ehrman and Dörnyei 1998:270), they quoted a comment that a trainee language teacher made after attending an introductory course on group dynamics:

> *To learn that ... classroom dynamics is not only an idealistic theory but something that even I myself can apply and work on consciously in my class was one of the best and most useful things during the whole of my university studies.*

This quote summarises our view of group dynamics: we feel that it is one of the – if not *the* – most useful academic subdisciplines for classroom practitioners. We can only hope that this book has provided evidence for this. In this concluding chapter we would like to focus on three things:

- Recapitulating briefly the main points from each chapter in a list format.
- Highlighting the need to consider the whole school environment and the dynamics of the staff/faculty.
- Bringing closure to this book and saying goodbye.

10.1 Brief summary

The following table contains the main points of the previous nine chapters. This list can serve as a reminder of the ideas and concepts we have covered, and you can also use it as a quick overview or review. However, there is one thing we would like to reiterate: although group dynamics is a well-researched discipline with established tenets and principles, we need to remember that groups are ultimately *dynamic* in nature and therefore the various principles cannot be applied blindly, without considering what stage the group is at and what its main needs are. Indeed, the key element of a group-sensitive approach is to be *sensitive*. Therefore, please regard the following list as a broad menu from which you can sample ideas in a flexible manner.

Furthermore, introducing group-building ideas needs to be a gradual process. You yourself cannot change at once and neither can the group. Perhaps the best thing to do is to start with one or two ideas and see how they work. Very soon you will (hopefully) notice some positive group response, which in turn will make the implementation of further ideas easier. And at one point (again, hopefully), you'll be able to sit back and relax even more because the group has taken over a great portion of your management and motivational work.

The principal ideas presented in the nine chapters

Chapter 1 Becoming a group

- Initial classes set interaction patterns and group structures that will form group life.
- Initial group life is emotionally loaded for both the students and the teacher.
- In order for a cohesive group to develop, the initial likes and dislikes should be replaced by acceptance among the students; the teacher can do a lot to facilitate this process.

Chapter 2 Managing the class: Rules, norms and discipline

- Certain 'rules of conduct' are necessary in the classroom to make joint learning possible.
- Rules and regulations set early in the group's life give it stability; for a group norm to be long-lasting and constructive, it needs to be accepted by the group.
- Group norms greatly facilitate the keeping of classroom discipline because you can count on the students to help you to enforce them.
- Conflicts between norms mandated by classes, institutions, and larger systems happen.

Chapter 3 How groups develop

- The typical stages of group life are formation, transition, performing and dissolution.
- The teacher can do a lot to help students navigate these changes.
- Some individuals might not be aligned perfectly with the group's trajectory.
- We find regular fluctuations of emotional distance and closeness amongst group members; however, the more mature the group

---

gets, the more the intensity of the fluctuation decreases and task effort stabilises.

- Groups sometimes do not go through the four basic stages of development or reach the mature performing phase: they may skip a stage or get stuck.

Chapter 4 The cohesive group: relationships and achievement

- Cohesiveness forms a good foundation upon which groups can become productive.
- There are many techniques available to promote group cohesiveness.
- Group life has two strands: socialisation and goal-oriented behaviour – the first supporting the second. However, some groups may cohere and permit socialisation to be their main task to the detriment of goal-oriented behaviour.
- Respect for the group and its members should not lead to uncritical 'groupthink'.

Chapter 5 The classroom environment's contribution to group dynamics

- There is a strong interplay between the group's physical environment and the dynamics in it.
- Components of the environment (what we see, hear, and feel) are always to a certain extent adaptable by the participants.
- Some of the features that are often available for change to enhance learning are:
    where students are located;
    the variety of partners they interact with;
    how often they change partners;
    the placement of the chairs (U-shape, circle, etc.);
    the classroom temperature and lighting;
    the décor;
    the feeling of ownership of the classroom;
    the movement of the teacher and students;
    the use of songs and music;
    leaving the classroom and going outside.

Chapter 6 The teacher as group leader

- Leadership matters; by becoming more aware of what effective leadership entails, we can lead our class groups more effectively.
- One leadership style is not necessarily better than another, it depends on what stage the group is at and what the group needs at certain moments in time.

- Generally, it is recommended that group-conscious teaching begins more *autocratically* to give direction, security, and impetus to the group. Then as the group begins performing, teachers initiate *democratic* processes. When students begin to show their initiative, more autonomy-inviting leadership is most productive for encouraging student independence and initiative.
- Empathy, acceptance and congruence are the three attributes of the effective facilitator.
- Rather than simply doing a job as a transactional leader, a *transformational* leader educates for life and motivates the group to perform beyond standard expectations of performance.
- Prerequisites to becoming more *transformational* in our leadership role include trust in the group, enthusiasm about the subject matter, commitment to the students' learning and skills in building rapport with them.
- One of the goals of an effective leader is to lead so well as to no longer be needed at times, generating student autonomy; scaffolding this can be done in many ways.

Chapter 7 Student roles and role modelling

- Student roles describe what learners are supposed to do. They can be informal, emerging naturally, and formal, assigned by the teacher.
- Roles are of great importance with regard to the life and productivity of the group.
- Teachers can increase the effectiveness and productivity of their classes by inviting or assigning specific student roles, short-circuiting the negative ones and promoting students' agency to develop in a variety of positive ways.
- In order to ensure that students perform their roles effectively, they must receive some explicit preparation.
- 'Near peer role models' are peers whom one may respect and admire; highlighting their productive behaviours, roles and beliefs can encourage students to follow the example.
- Near peer role modelling methods (newsletters, videoing and language learner histories) use the excellence already present in the group to help it become more cohesive and performative.

Chapter 8 Trouble-shooting: Conflicts and apathy happen!

- Conflict is natural and inevitable in human relations.
- Conflict can have positive functions in the life of a group.
- Effective group-building strategies early in a group's life make conflict less frequent and less trenchant.

- Strategies to handle conflict effectively can be taught, practised and learned.
- Teachers need not panic when there are conflicts or low points in group-life; very often these are natural concomitants of group-life that every healthy group undergoes.
- Most conflicts can be dealt with openly (and of course sensitively) – suppressing them will usually not make them go away.
- We should have enough trust in our groups to assume that it can cope with its problems. The teacher doesn't have to always *solve* them, but rather bring them up for discussion.
- Some apathy may occur in any group in the cycle of their learning; increasing goal-orientedness and applying other motivational strategies may be effective in livening up the class.

Chapter 9 The last classes: Affirming and closing
- An appropriately conscious closure affects students' present state and future learning.
- Affirming what has gone on in the class serves an important instructional function and it also helps to leave a positive impression of the group experience.
- Teachers can attend to the swelling of separation anxiety and create healthy emotional closure by allowing and encouraging the open expressions of students' feelings.
- Projecting into the future will help students think about life after the group and be prepared for living beyond the group.
- The teacher's requests for student feedback about the course can serve the double purpose of preparing closure and providing valuable information to the teacher for professional development.

10.2 The need to consider the whole school environment

In Chapter 2 we already mentioned briefly that even the best intentions and the most skilful group-building practice might not be successful in an inhospitable environment. If there is an inconsistency between the school's 'hidden curriculum' and the classroom's desired norm system, the resulting dissonance can undermine some of our best efforts. Therefore, it may be difficult to develop and sustain changes in the classroom without dealing with the wider school environment (Ehrman and Dörnyei 1998; Murphey and Sato 2000). Let us reiterate Schmuck and Schmuck's (1997) conclusion about this issue (already quoted in Chapter 2), because it says it all: 'Attempts to improve classroom group processes often should be either accompanied or preceded by attempts to improve the group processes of the staff' (p. 248).

So, it is beneficial that while you are trying to implement changes in your classrooms, you also talk to your colleagues (and even the school management) about your ideas in order to bring them on board. You'll find that you are not alone: other teachers are also facing problems similar to the ones you are trying to cope with. You can think and dream together. Indeed, we suggest that you try and develop some positive dynamics in the staff group. After all, the processes you would like to promote among the students may work best when they are reflected by similar processes at the staff level. And this is not just an optimistic assumption but something that has been supported by research. Let us summarise here a fascinating study by Susan Wheelan and Felice Tilin (1999).

The inspiration for Wheelan and Tilin's study was provided by various reports in the literature concluding that the level of development and collegiality of school staff groups is positively related to the effectiveness of the school and the achievement of the students. As the authors point out, in the educational literature the adjective 'collegial' has been used to refer to staff and faculty who work together effectively, who share common goals, professional values and norms. More specifically, collegiality can be defined in terms of four behaviours of the adults in a school:

- having frequent conversations about teaching and learning;
- observing and providing feedback for one another;
- working collaboratively on the curriculum;
- teaching one another about teaching, learning and leading.

In order to test the validity of these reports, Wheelan and Tilin set out to examine the relationship between staff/faculty group effectiveness and the actual level of productivity in ten American elementary, middle and high schools. Their results fully confirmed that a strong relationship exists between staff/faculty group functioning and student outcomes. In group developmental terms, schools with faculty groups operating at higher levels of group development had students who performed better on standard achievement tests both in maths and reading. This points to the conclusion that the quality of the teaching a school can provide is related to the maturity and collegiality level of the staff/faculty group.

We suspect that these group influences also work at the city, district and national levels. A cohesive and well-functioning local education authority or a department of education that has a work culture characterised by open communication, rewards for risk-taking (not necessarily success) and a mission that is well-communicated would seem to be closing in on group dynamic nirvana. Although these are undoubtedly exciting and significant issues, we have to leave the study of group dynamics at these macro levels for now. It is something that we, as authors, may be looking at more closely in the near future.

10.3 Parting words

The endings of movies, the endings of stories, the endings of classes, all need closure. Rather than just letting the end happen with a disturbing vacuity, seeing a class and its development as a story that twists and turns in mysterious ways and at some moment ends may allow us to consciously choose and influence our endings, and make the most of them. Even living with a good book for a while can bring with it a sense of sadness at closure and a sense of satisfaction with achievement. When we feel only a few pages left, some of us thumb through the last few pages and look briefly at the last line and think to ourselves that it has been a good book. Then we go back and read those last few pages. Why wait for the future to be nostalgic about today? Plan to enjoy it now – with a few tears, a hug, a handshake, and a long look in the eyes. And a fare thee well. Until we meet again.

Zoltán and Tim

You are invited . . .

We are curious about what you think about the ideas we have presented in this book and how they have actually worked in your classes. Would you consider sharing your experiences with us? We learn with you. Your stories will allow us to ground the theory in practice and to be more relevant to the concerns of teachers in the classroom. When you wish to, we welcome your correspondence. If enough people are interested, we may form an internet list in which everyone could discuss these issues more openly and fully. We certainly would like the discussion to continue. Thank you!

Contact information:
- Zoltán: zoltan.dornyei@nottingham.ac.uk
- Tim: mits@dokkyo.ac.jp

References

Aoki, N. 1999. Affect and the role of teachers in the development of learner autonomy. In J. Arnold (Ed.), *Affective Language Learning*. Cambridge: Cambridge University Press, 142–154.

Arnold, J. (Ed.) 1999. *Affective Language Learning*. Cambridge: Cambridge University Press.

Atwater, D. C. and B. M. Bass 1994. Transformational leadership in teams. In B. M. Bass and B. J. Avolio (Eds.), *Improving Organizational Effectiveness through Transformational Leadership*. Thousand Oaks, CA: Sage, 48–83.

Awane, N. 2002. A study of good and bad groups. Unpublished seminar paper. School of English Studies, University of Nottingham.

Bailey, K., B. Berghold, B. Braunstein, N. Fleischman, M. Holbrook, J. Turman, X. Waissbluth and L. Zambo 1996. The language learner's autobiography: Examining the 'apprenticeship of observation.' In D. Freeman and J. C. Richards (Eds.), *Teacher Learning in Language Teaching*. New York, NY: Cambridge Universtiy Press, 11–29.

Bailey, K., A. Curtis and D. Nunan 2001. *Pursuing Professional Development*. Boston, MA: Heinle and Heinle.

Bandura, A. 1997. *Self-Efficacy: The Exercise of Control*. New York: Freeman.

Bass, B. M. and B. J. Avolio (Eds.) 1994. *Improving Organizational Effectiveness through Transformational Leadership*. Thousand Oaks, CA: Sage.

Benson, P. 2001. *Teaching and Researching Autonomy in Language Learning*. Harlow: Longman.

Bolstad, R and M. Hamblett 1997. *Transforming Communication*. Auckland: Addison Wesley Longman.

Brandes, D. and P. Ginnis 1986. *A Guide to Student-Centred Learning*. Oxford: Blackwell.

Brophy, J. E. 1998. *Motivating Students to Learn*. Boston, MA: McGraw-Hill.

Brown, H. D. 1994. *Teaching by Principles*. Englewood Cliffs, NJ: Prentice Hall.

Brown, R. 2000. *Group Processes: Dynamics Within and Between Groups* (2nd ed.). Oxford: Blackwell.

Brumfit, C. J. 1984. *Communicative Methodology in Language Teaching: The Roles of Fluency and Accuracy*. Cambridge: Cambridge University Press.

Buzaglo, G. and S. A. Wheelan 1999. Facilitating work team effectiveness: Case studies from Central America. *Small Group Research*, 30, 108–129.

Clément, R., Z. Dörnyei and K. A. Noels 1994. Motivation, self-confidence and group cohesion in the foreign language classroom. *Language Learning*, 44, 417–448.

Cohen, E. 1994. *Designing Groupwork* (2nd ed.). New York: Teachers College Press.

Costa Guerra, V. (2002). Group dynamics research project. Unpublished seminar paper. School of English Studies, University of Nottingham.

Covey, S. 1989. *The 7 Habits of Highly Effective People*. New York, Simon & Schuster.

Crum, T. F. 1987. *The Magic of Conflict: Turning a Life of Work into a Work of Art*. New York: Simon and Schuster.

Csikszentmihalyi, M. 1997. Intrinsic motivation and effective teaching: A flow analysis. In J. L. Bess (Ed.), *Teaching Well and Liking It: Motivating Faculty to Teach Effectively*. Baltimore: Johns Hopkins University Press, 72–89.

De Souza, G. and H. J. Klein 1995. Emergent leadership in the group goal-setting process. *Small Group Research*, 26, 475–496.

Dörnyei, Z. 1990. Csoportdinamika és nyelvoktatás [Group dynamics in language teaching]. *Pedagógiai Szemle*, 40, 307–318.

Dörnyei, Z. 1995. Student participation in different types of classroom interaction tasks: A longitudinal investigation. In S. Rot (Ed.), *Studies in English and American, Vol. 7*. Budapest: Eötvös University, 213–218.

Dörnyei, Z. 1997. Psychological processes in cooperative language learning: Group dynamics and motivation. *Modern Language Journal*, 81, 482–493.

Dörnyei, Z. 2001a. *Teaching and Researching Motivation*. Harlow: Longman.

Dörnyei. Z. 2001b. *Motivational Strategies in the Language Classroom*. Cambridge: Cambridge University Press.

Dörnyei, Z. 2003. *Questionnaires in Second Language Research: Construction, Administration and Processing*. Mahwah, NJ: Lawrence Erlbaum.

Dörnyei, Z. and K. Gajdátsy 1989a. A student-centred approach to language learning 1. *Practical English Teaching*, 9/3, 43–45.

Dörnyei, Z. and K. Gajdátsy 1989b. A student-centred approach to language learning 2. *Practical English Teaching*, 9/4, 34–35.

Dörnyei, Z. and A. Malderez 1997. Group dynamics and foreign language teaching. *System*, 25, 65–81.

Dörnyei, Z. and A. Malderez 1999. Group dynamics in foreign language learning and teaching. In J. Arnold (Ed.), *Affective Language Learning*. Cambridge: Cambridge University Press, 155–169.

Ehrman, M. E. and Z. Dörnyei 1998. *Interpersonal Dynamics in Second Language Education: The Visible and Invisible Classroom*. Thousand Oaks, CA: Sage.

Ekbatani, G. and H. Pierson (Eds.) 2000. *Learner-Directed Assessment in ESL*. Mahwah, NJ: Lawrence Erlbaum.

Foels, R., J. E. Driskell, B. Mullen and E. Salas. 2000. The effects of democratic leadership on group member satisfaction. *Small Group Research*, 31, 676–701.

Forsyth, D. R. 1999. *Group Dynamics* (3rd ed.). Pacific Grove, CA: Brooks/ Cole.

Frank, C. and M. Rinvolucri 1991. *Grammar in Action Again: Awareness Activities for Language Learning*. Hemel Hempstead: Prentice Hall.

Gibbons, P. 2002. *Scaffolding Language, Scaffolding Learning: Teaching Second Language Learners in the Mainstream Classroom*. Portsmouth, NH: Heinemann.

Hadfield, J. 1992. *Classroom Dynamics*. Oxford: Oxford University Press.

Harrist, A. W. and K. D. Bradley 2002. Social exclusion in the classroom: Teachers and students as agents of change. In J. Aronson (Ed.), *Improving Academic Achievement: Impact of Psychological Factors on Education*. San Diago, CA: Academic Press, 363–383.

Heron, J. 1999. *The Complete Facilitator's Handbook*. London: Kogan Page.

Hersey, P. and K. H. Blanchard 1982. *Management of Organizational Behavior* (4th ed.). Englewood Cliffs, NJ: Prentice-Hall.

Hook, P. and A. Vass 2000. *Confident Classroom Leadership*. London: David Fulton.

Johnson, D. W. and R. T. Johnson 1995. Cooperative Learning and non-academic outcomes of schooling: The other side of the report card. In J. E. Pedersen and A. D. Digby (Eds.), *Secondary Schools and Cooperative Learning*. New York: Garland, 3–54.

Johnson, D. W. and R. T. Johnson 2000. *Joining Together: Group theory and group skills* (7th ed.). Boston, MA: Allyn and Bacon.

Jones, V. F. and L. S. Jones 2000. *Comprehensive Classroom Management: Creating Communities of Support and Solving Problems* (6th ed.). Needham Heights, MA: Allyn and Bacon.

Jordan, D. J. 2001. *Leisure leadership in leisure services: Making a difference* (2nd ed.). State College, PN: Venture Publishing.

Jung D. I. and J. J. Sosik 2002. Transformational leadership in work groups: The role of empowerment, cohesiveness and collective efficacy on perceived group performance. *Small Group Research*, 33, 313–336.

Kellerman, H. 1981. The deep structures of group cohesion. In H. Kellerman (Ed.), *Group Cohesion: Theoretical and Clinical Perspectives*. New York: Grune and Stratton, 3–21.

Kemp, T. and A. Taylor 1992. *The Groupwork Pack*. Harlow: Longman.

Kenny, T. 1994. Does remembering a student's name effect student performance? *Nanzan's LT Briefs* 1/2, 3.

Kenny, T. 1995. How to easily remember student names. *Nanzan's LT Briefs* 2/1.

Kindt, D. 2001. String Toss. *English Teaching Professional*, 20, 39.

Koui, S. 2002. Group dynamics in two Greek state schools. Unpublished seminar paper. School of English Studies, University of Nottingham.

Kushida, Y. 1995. Near peer role models. Unpublished senior thesis. Nanzan University, Department of American and British Studies.

Lambert, N. M. 1994. Seating arrangements in classrooms. In *International Encyclopedia of Education* (2nd ed., Vol. 9). Oxford: Pergamon, 5355–5359.

Larsen-Freeman, D. 2000. *Techniques and Principles in Language Teaching* (2nd ed.). Oxford: Oxford University Press.

Legutke, M. and Thomas, H. 1994. *Process and Experience in the Language Classroom*. New York: Longman.

Levi, D. 2001. *Group Dynamics for Teams*. Thousand Oaks, CA: Sage.

Levine, J. M. and R. L. Moreland 1990. Progress in small group research. *Annual Review of Psychology*, 41, 585–6340.

Levine, J. M. and R. L. Moreland 1998. Small groups. In D. T. Gilbert, S. T. Fiske and G. Lindzey (Eds.), *Handbook of Social Psychology* (4th ed., Vol. 2). Boston, MA: McGraw-Hill, 415–469.

Lewin, K., R. Lippitt and R. White 1939. Patterns of aggressive behavior in experimentally created 'social climate'. *Journal of Psychology*, 10, 271–299.

Lin, M-L. 2002. Group dynamics project. Unpublished seminar paper. School of English Studies, University of Nottingham.

Long, M. H. and P. A. Porter 1985. Group work, interlanguage talk and second language acquisition. *TESOL Quarterly*, 19, 207–228.

Luft, J. 1984. *Group Processes: An Introduction to Group Dynamics* (3rd ed.). Palo Alto, CA: Mayfield Publishing.

Malderez, A. and C. Bodóczky, C. 1999. *Mentor Courses: A Resource Book for Teacher Trainers*. Cambridge: Cambridge University Press.

Maley, A. and A. Duff 1982. *Drama Techniques in Language Learning* (2nd ed.). Cambridge: Cambridge University Press.

McCollom, M. 1990. Group formation: Boundaries, leadership and culture. In J. Gilette and M. McCollom (Eds.), *Groups in Context: A New Perspective on Group Dynamics*. Reading, MA: Addison-Wesley, 35–48.

McCombs, B. L. and J. E. Pope 1994. *Motivating Hard to Reach Students*. Washington DC: American Psychological Association.

McCombs, B. L. and J. S. Whisler 1997. *The Learner-Centered Classroom and School: Strategies for Increasing Student Motivation and Achievement*. San Francisco, CA: Jossey-Bass.

McCormick, F. G. Jr. 1994. *The Power of Positive Teaching*. Malabar, FL: Krieger.

MacLennan, B. W. and K. S. Dies 1992. *Group Counseling and Psychotherapy with Adolescents* (2nd ed.). New York: Columbia University.

Medgyes, P. 2001a. *The Non-Native Teacher*. Ismaning, Germany: Max Huebner Verlag.

Medgyes, P. 2001b. When the teacher is a non-native speaker. In M. Celce-Murcia (Ed.), *Teaching English as a Foreign Language* (3rd ed.). Boston, MA: Heinle & Heinle, 429–442.

Mullen, B. and Copper, C. 1994. The relation between group cohesiveness and performance: An integration. *Psychological Bulletin*, 115, 210–227.

Murphey, T. 1977. Crazy TOEFL. *TESOL Newsletter*, 11/5, 7.

Murphey, T. 1991. *Teaching One to One*. Harlow: Longman.

Murphey, T. 1993. Why don't teachers learn what learners learn? Taking the guesswork out with Action Logging. *English Teaching Forum*, 31(2), 6–10.

Murphey, T. 1994. Tests: Learning through negotiated interaction. *TESOL Journal*, 3, 12–16.

Murphey, T. 1995. Action Logging. In R. White (Ed.), *New Ways in Teaching Writing*. Alexandria, VA: TESOL, 213–214.

Murphey, T. 1996. Changing language learning beliefs: 'Appreshiating' mistakes. *Asian Journal of English Language Teaching*, 6, 77–84.

Murphey, T. 1997. Learning what learners learn: Action Logging. In D. Brinton and P. Master (Eds.), *New Ways in Content-Based Instruction*. Alexandria, VA: TESOL, 144–145.

Murphey, T. 1998a. *Language Hungry! an introduction to language learning fun and self-esteem*. Tokyo: Macmillan Languagehouse.

Murphey, T. 1998b. Friends and classroom identity formation. *IATEFL Issues*, 145, 15–16.

Murphey, T. 1998c. Motivating with near peer role models. In B. Visgatis (Ed.), *On JALT '97: Trends and Transitions*. Tokyo: JALT, 205–209.

Murphey, T. 1998d. *Language Learning Histories I*. Nagoya: South Mountain Press.

Murphey, T. 1998e. *Language Learning Histories II*. Nagoya: South Mountain Press.

Murphey, T. 1999. Publishing students' language learning histories: For them, their peers and their teachers. *Between the Keys (Newsletter of the JALT Material Writers SIG)*, 7, 8–11,14.

Murphey, T. 2000. *Shadowing and Summarizing* (NFLRC Video #11). Honolulu: University of Hawai'i, NFLRC. Order: http://nflrc.hawaii.edu/publication_home.cfm

Murphey, T. 2001a. Tools of recursion, intermental zones of proximal development and critical collaborative autonomy. *JALT Journal*, 23, 130–150.

Murphey, T. 2001b. Videoing conversations for self-evalutation in Japan. In J. Murphy and P. Byrd (Eds.), *Understanding the Courses we Teach: Local Perspectives on English Language Teaching*. Ann Arbor: University of Michigan Press, 179–196.

Murphey, T. (Ed.) 2003. *Narrativizing Teaching: Socializing Ourselves into Practice*. Hsin Chu, Taiwan: South Mountain Press.

Murphey, T. 2003. *Near Peer Role Modeling* (NFLRC Video #14). Honolulu: University of Hawai'i NFLRC. Order: http://nflrc.hawaii.edu/publication_home.cfm

Murphey, T. and H. Arao 2001. Changing reported beliefs through near peer role modeling. *TESL-EJ*, 5(3), 115.

Murphey, T. and G. Jacobs 2000. Encouraging critical collaborative autonomy. *JALT Journal*, 22, 228–244.

Murphey, T. and K. Murakami 1998. Near peer role models for changing beliefs. *Academia*, 65, 1–29.

Murphey, T. and K. Sato 2000. Enhancing teacher development: What administrators can do. *The Language Teacher*, 24/1, 7–10.

Nyikos, M. and R. Oxford (Eds.) 1997. Interaction, collaboration and co-operation: Learning languages and preparing language teachers. Special Issue. *Modern Language Journal*, 81/4.

Oxford, R. and Green, J. 1996. Language learning histories: learners and teachers helping each other understand learning styles and strategies. *TESOL Journal*, 5, 20–23.

Oyster, C. K. 2000. *Groups: A User's Guide*. Boston, MA: McGraw-Hill.

Ozawa, T. 2002. Community building strategies for junior high school English classes. Unpublished MA thesis. Nanzan University, Japan.

Palincsar, A. S. and A. L. Brown 1984. Reciprocal teaching of comprehension-fostering and comprehension-monitoring activities. *Cognition and Instruction*, 1, 117–175.

Pawan, F. and A. Jacobson. In press. Growing with the flow: Sustaining professionalism through online instruction of language teachers. In T. Murphey (Ed.), *Extending Professional Contributions*. Arlington, VA: TESOL.

Pruitt, D. G. 1998. Social conflict. In D. T. Gilbert, S. T. Fiske and G. Lindzey (Eds.), *The Handbook of Social Psychology* (4th ed., Vol. 2). Boston, MA: McGraw-Hill, 470–503.

Rogers, C. R. 1961. *On Becoming a Person*. Boston, MA: Houghton Mifflin.

Rogers, C. R. 1970. *Carl Rogers on Encounter Groups*. New York: Harper and Row.

Rogers, C. R. 1983. *Freedom to Learn for the 80s*. Columbus, OH: Merrill.

Rosenthal, R. and L. Jacobson 1968. *Pygmalion in the Classroom*. New York: Holt, Rinehart and Winston.

Schmuck R. A. and P. A. Schmuck 1997. *Group Processes in the Classroom* (7th ed.). Dubuque, IA: Brown and Benchmark.

Schmuck R. A. and P. A. Schmuck 2001. *Group Processes in the Classroom* (8th ed.). Boston, MA: McGraw-Hill.

Schumann, J. H. 1998. *The Neurobiology of Affect in Language*. Oxford: Blackwell.

Senior, R. 1996. Teachers' craft knowledge: The importance of developing a positive group feeling in language classrooms. In G. Tinker Sachs, M. Brock and R. Lo (Eds.), *Directions in Second Language Teacher Education*. Hong Kong: City University of Hong Kong, 97–106.

Senior, R. 1997. Transforming language classes into bonded groups. *ELT Journal*, 51, 3–11.

Senior, R. 2002. A class-centred approach to language teaching. *ELT Journal*, 56, 397–403.

Shambaugh, P. W. 1978. The development of the small group. *Human Relations*, 31, 283–295.

Shamim, F. 1996. In or out of the action zone: Location as a feature of interaction in large ESL classes in Pakistan. In K. M. Bailey and D. Nunan (Eds.), *Voices from the language classroom*. Cambridge: Cambridge University Press, 123–144.

Shaw, M. E. 1981. *Group Dynamics: The Psychology of Small Group Behavior* (3rd ed.). New York: McGraw-Hill.

Sherif, M. 1966. *Group Conflict and Co-operation*. London: Routledge and Kegan Paul.

Stevick, E. W. 1980 *Teaching Languages: A Way and Ways*. Rowley, MA: Newbury House.

Stevick, E. W. 1990. *Humanism in Language Teaching*. Oxford: Oxford University Press.

Stewart, G. L., C. C. Manz and H. P. Sims Jr. 1999. *Team Work and Group Dynamics*. New York: John Wiley and Sons.

Tiberius, R. G. 1999. *Small Group Teaching: A Trouble-Shooting Guide*. London: Kogan Page.

Triantafyllopoulou, A. 2002. Group dynamics in a Greek educational context. Unpublished seminar paper. School of English Studies, University of Nottingham.

Turner, J. C. 1984. Social identification and psychological group formation. In H. Tajfel (Ed.), *The Social Dimension: European Studies in Social Psychology*. Cambridge: Cambridge University Press and Paris: Editions de la Maison des Sciences de l'Homme, 518–538.

Underhill, A. 1999. Facilitation in language teaching. In J. Arnold (Ed.), *Affective Language Learning*. Cambridge: Cambridge University Press, 125–141.

Usui, T. 2002. Research into student experiences of good and bad groups. Unpublished seminar paper. School of English Studies, University of Nottingham.

Vygotsky, L. 1962. *Thought and Language*. Cambridge, MA: MIT Press.

Vygotsky, L. 1978. *Mind in Society: The Development of Higher Psychological Processes*. Cambridge, MA: Harvard University Press.

Wheelan, S. A. 1994. *Group Process: A Developmental Perspective*. Boston, MA: Allyn and Bacon.

Wheelan, S. A. 1999. Introduction to this special issue on group development. *Small Group Research*, 30, 3–7.

Wheelan, S. A. and F. Tilin 1999. The relationship between faculty group development and school productivity. *Small Group Research*, 30, 59–81.

Williams, M. and R. Burden 1997. *Psychology for Language Teachers*. Cambridge: Cambridge University Press.

Wilson, G. L. 2002. *Groups in Context: Leadership and Participation in Small Groups* (6th ed.). Boston, MA: McGraw-Hill.

Woo, L. and T. Murphey 1999. Activating metacognition with action logs. *The Language Teacher*, 23, 15–18.

Yalom, I. 1995. *The Theory and Practice of Group Psychotherapy*. (4th ed.). New York: Basic.

Yamashita, Y. 1998. Near peer role modeling in language learning histories. Unpublished senior thesis. Nanzan University, Department of American and British Studies.

Yoneyama, S. 1999. *The Japanese High School: Silence and Resistance*. London: Routledge.

Index